What If I Whispered Your Name?

Anne Pieterse

Copyright © 2011 by Anne Pieterse.

www.intimacythroughgrief.com

Library of Congress Control Number:		2011906735
ISBN:	Softcover	978-1-4628-5741-8
	Ebook	978-1-4628-5742-5

All rights reserved. No part of this book may be reproduced or transmitted in any form or by any means, electronic or mechanical, including photocopying, recording, or by any information storage and retrieval system, without permission in writing from the copyright owner.

This book was printed in the United States of America.

To order additional copies of this book, contact:
Xlibris Corporation
0-800-644-6988
www.xlibrispublishing.co.uk
Orders@Xlibrispublishing.co.uk
301904

Contents

In Gratitude 9

Introduction 11

Chapter One – Anchored Grief of the Past 17

Chapter Two – Gone forever 20

Chapter Three – Shock 23

Chapter Four – The Insensitive things people say: 25

Chapter Five – Betrayal 28

Chapter Six – Finding Intimacy 35

Chapter Seven – Is there a God? 38

Chapter Eight – Hope—Spiritual Alchemy 41

Chapter Nine – Finding Direction through Symbolism 43

Chapter Ten – My 5 Seasons of Grief 47

Chapter Eleven – Changing Tides 53

Chapter Twelve – Acceptance and Letting Go 58

Chapter Thirteen – Revisiting Grief 61

Chapter Fourteen – Transformation through Creativity 70

Chapter Fifteen – Epilogue:Staring Death in the Face 74

Chapter Sixteen – Miracles 80

Chapter Seventeen – Survival 90

This book is dedicated to my children

Kristo

***

Jason and Sarah,
the reason I am here today! xxx

In Gratitude

'Oriah'

I thought I was on the edge until
'You pushed me further'

Many rich blessings

"The Invitation" is by Oriah from her book

THE INVITATION (c) 1999.
Published by HarperONE, San Francisco.

All rights reserved. Presented with
permission of the Author—www.oriah.org

Introduction

"If tears could build a stairway,
And memories a lane,
I'd walk right up to Heaven
And bring you home again".

~ Unknown

What is Grief?

Grief is an inescapable reality of our human experience and existence. Grief is a collection of feelings and behaviors, and a reflection on the connection to what we have lost.

At moments of profound loss, our defences crumble. We no longer have the energy to hide our feelings or shut them out. Grieving is one of the most difficult and painful experiences we go through in our lives. It challenges us mentally, physically, spiritually and emotionally to the limit. Our lives will not return to the normality we had before our loss, but we will adjust and find our new normal selves. The loss of a child is one of the hardest and most devastating and traumatic experiences a parent can go through.

My Journey

I am going to take you on my own personal journey, working through my feelings moment by moment, and will explain to you how I faced the many obstacles that grief put in my way. Grief is what we feel, and grieving is what we do, after we have lost someone dear to us. After a long while—about a year or so later—I chose to face and try to embrace my grief instead of fighting it. I trust that by intimately sharing my journey, of grief with you, that you too may understand that you are not alone on your path and there are many avenues open for you to follow, and resources out there to help you. Many of us in grief prefer to stay at home in the early stages and never venture out in fear of someone asking us how our loved one is. This is our worst nightmare after losing our dear one and we all dread this, or the comments that may be made. How would we cope, what would we say? More importantly, how would we react? Although I did not want to join any group, I found 'The Compassionate Friends' a safe haven to go to in my time of grief. They provided me with the tools and skills of how to deal with certain situations, especially anniversary dates, birthdays, special occasions, and their support has been invaluable. You never need to be alone or isolated in your grief unless you choose to be. To be honest, for weeks I just sat in the meetings and listened until I found the courage to talk if my voice allowed.

Watching our beloved son 'Kristo' being swept out to sea was the beginning of many years of grief and healing. I can replay this 'scene' over and over again like a real life, panoramic color motion picture, especially if a trigger such as the anniversary of his death sets me off. I have learnt how to shut this away, as it is a painful place and not one I should reflect on all the time. We spend a lot of time reflecting on the actual death itself and the circumstances around it, instead of the life our loved ones spent with us and all the precious memories and moments we shared together. We remember very little of our son from the years before his death; the trauma has been too great.

I will also be sharing with you my '5 Seasons of Grief' which explain the different seasons I need to journey through, back and forth. Knowing exactly which season I am likening to helps me understand myself more fully and allows me to work through my own emotions and feelings. This self awareness allows me to shift between the seasons and not become particularly stuck in a season.

My path has not been an easy one, as there have been many triggers that lead me to remember. They are in our everyday lives, especially when I hear of children missing, freak waves, tsunamis, and the force and anger of Mother Nature. I know what death feels like, I know what 'missing' feels like, and I know what the wrath of Mother Nature looks and feels like too. Triggers take us back to revisit the event, or we can have 'flashbacks' most unexpectedly, even if we don't want them.

This is a very personal narrative, and includes my own perceptions and true stories. Although my story may appear narcissistic at times, I am explaining grief and sorrow from my own heart as a mother. Every journey of grief is different, and every journey is sacred. No two people's grief is the same, and nobody's grief should be hurried by external pressure, nor judged by anyone.

I am dedicating this book to those who have lost a child or children and who may feel lost and lonely at this very time. We tend to put up a barrier after the death of a loved one. We won't let anybody in for fear of more hurt and pain. We shut the most important people out of our lives, but in doing so we are just hurting ourselves more.

It may be that you are facing your own illness, or that of your child, partner, parents, friend or someone very close to you; it may be terminal, it may not be. You may be facing your own mortality, or you could have an altered body image. In every event, the path of grief is the same. You may not want to face the road ahead, you may not know how to. I have found that there is a common thread that weaves through us while we are on our path of grief, whether it be before or after a death—the only aspect that varies is the depth. If we are diagnosed with an incurable illness, we still need to go through the stages of grief and find our own acceptance in our own way. In death we are separated from someone we treasured and loved, and we will be separated forever.

To be in such emotional and physical pain, we must have truly loved someone dear to us. We have a longing to resume that connection and to be with our loved one if only for one split second. Grief is not an illness, and we cannot cure or hurry it or its process. There is no rush; you need to be very gentle, kind and patient with yourself.

There are many factors which contribute to how long we take to grieve, and this varies according to who or what we have lost, our past history, and any 'anchored grief' or 'unfinished business' that we may have had before a new grief arrives.

There is no right or wrong way to experience grief, and grief will take as long as it takes. It may take forever. If we have any business that was 'unfinished' before this new wave of grief hits, we will be taken back to it time and time again until we have completed the process completely. We are all different and unique, and grief is a process that needs to be worked through in order to achieve a positive and healthy outcome.

I have experienced many deaths in our immediate family circle, including a drowning, car accident, murder and natural deaths. I have worked through the multitudes of grief that these have all presented. I have touched my own sorrow many times and still do today, but it is now manageable. There are triggers everywhere, and you are more aware of these after you have lost someone very dear to you. I have somehow still managed to cope with all of these deaths and remain 'sane' enough to stay married and bring up my two remaining children the eldest who was born with an incurable genetic disease, Cystic Fibrosis and needed continuous care. Care-giver, nurse, mum and motivator—I am all these, and fulfill all the responsibilities a grieving parent still needs to.

The ongoing loss I experienced, first starting with the death of Kristo, and then one immediate family member per year over the next five years, felt like waves of grief smashing over me. I felt like an innocent rock in the sea being smashed by wave after wave. More recently, in the last year, I experienced the near-death of my eldest son, who, during the terminal stages of his disease, received donor organs that failed, and he was then placed on total life support. He was placed on 'ECMO' (heart lung machine) as his blood needed to be transported outside of his body to be oxygenated and then pumped back into him as his lungs had failed and his heart also needed supporting. Jason was given the 'last rites' on four separate occasions to prepare his soul for death.

I remember watching as the flat line on the heart-rate monitor set off the alarms and I was-moved away while they used a defibrillator to jump his heart back into rhythm again. He was miraculously saved at the last minute, which just happened to be on the eve of 'Our Lady of Lourdes Day'. The miracle unfolded before my eyes. Was there any coincidence? No. I just 'let be and let God'. I could not worry or stress anymore, it wouldn't help and would just exhaust me more. I signed the mountains of paperwork agreeing to the second transplant, and after him being anointed by the priest I said my very last goodbyes and stumbled back to my room as tears of sorrow from deep within my soul washed over my body. Saving his life was out of my hands now. I needed to face reality and accept the outcome, whatever it would be.

The many long, lonely hours of anxious anticipation I faced through the course of his last transplant surgery, and ongoing months of challenges and respiratory failure felt like forever. But he has miraculously gone on to survive! I have been challenged and tested to the limit.

Emotional intimacy becomes magical when we can trust and have confidence in others who are in similar situations and share a common ground. This intimacy nurtures us as we develop a greater insight into each other's innermost selves. This intimacy which includes sharing any guilt feelings we may have, allows healing to take place. It may not be appropriate to share your feelings with your partner / husband / wife / friend. You may feel that you are not able to share this type of intimacy with them or they may no longer be with you.

You may find it more helpful to look for support elsewhere, whether it be in grief groups, internet groups, friends, books or the trust of a grief counsellor.

Sometimes you may feel that your friends and family are tired of hearing about your grief and pain, as you tend to talk about it repeatedly because there is nothing else to talk about. If this is the case, joining a Support Group can be very helpful, as you get the opportunity to see that others are going through the same feelings and emotions that you are experiencing.

Chapter One

ANCHORED GRIEF OF THE PAST

"There are things that we don't want to happen but have to accept,
things we don't want to know but have to learn, and people we can't
live without but have to let go" ~ Unknown

It was only after the death of my youngest son that my whole world fell apart, and many 'old anchored grief's of the past came storming towards me, wave upon wave. I would first need to deal with the old anchored grief before I could focus on the grief that was before me.

It really took me ages to acknowledge what I was grieving about, as I kept trying to change the subject. I was grieving the loss of everything; I was lost in grief. I think I was playing for time, and that this was a mechanism to ease the pain I was feeling. I kept pushing the new grief away. Little did I know that this was because I had not worked through the earlier grief and sorrow of my life.

When 'Pandora's Box' finally opened, what was uncovered was years of pent up grief and emotions I had experienced from a very young age. Something inside of me had died a long time ago. My family had also separated when I was nine years old and I was torn away from those closest to me. I would very seldom ever see my father and three brothers again.

During our adult years, after we had all gotten married and had children, at about the same time, we bonded a little as the children/

17

cousins wanted to be together. However, we have lost the early bond that siblings make. Our relationships are dysfunctional and this is where my heartache begins. This is not what I want or wanted. I have tried to rekindle these relationships, but with great difficulty and little success. We are on speaking terms, but it's the special sibling kinship that's gone, and it's exactly that for which I ache. I am not bothered where they live or what they do, I just long to have a relationship with my brothers. I envy those who have a loving relationship. It would be nice to have just the odd phone call, an email or something intimate. It was so early on that I was divorced from my family, all four of them, and I felt very alone at the time. I never realised the damage this would cause, nor the long term effect it would have on me. I had never dealt with the grief and pain that this had caused, and was not even aware that it was there, but when I lost my son, that anchored grief of the past decided to come back to visit me most unexpectedly.

Due to my 'anchored grief', and not releasing stored-up energy that had accumulated through my younger life, I was a 'pressure cooker' of emotions waiting to explode. This would come back to haunt me when I was 17-years-old and nearing the end of my schooling. I was desperately ill in hospital. The doctor's couldn't find anything wrong with me but I lay motionless in my hospital bed for what would turn out to be a period of in and out of Hospital for three long months. I went through many dark nights of the soul and every inch of my body ached. I was unable to walk, I could not keep any food or liquids down. I was too weak to bath and was bed bathed. I was on a permanent IV replacement fluids.

At the time, I was going out with a man who would turn out to be my first husband. He visited me daily in hospital and was my soulmate at the time. I never got to finish the end of my school career, as I was too ill and grew thinner and thinner and weaker and weaker. Something inside me had snapped like a stick. I think now that it may subconsciously have been the thought of getting too close to someone I could lose. I was terrified of any more pain. Pain was not my friend. When I look back, I can see what my problem was even though at that stage I had no idea. This trigger had left me paralysed. I was not aware that I had internalised all of my pain and it was shutting me down.

I went on to marry my first husband when I was 20, had a beautiful son Jason at the age of 23, and got divorced a few years later. I only knew divorce and I only knew how to run from pain and betrayal. I have no regrets now, and that was a stepping stone to my next marriage.

Soon after my divorce, I met my second husband. He entered my life and that of Jason, who was 3 at the time, and embraced us for who we are. He is a humble man, although can at times be extremely difficult and stubborn. Together we had a beautiful son 'Kristo'. The pediatrician at the time told me I had been blessed with an 'angel'. He truly was, and too good for this earth. He was the only contented baby in the nursery at the hospital and never cried. He had a soft and gentle nature and was just a beautiful child; never moaned and was serene and special—just what I needed.

My first son Jason was like a 'firecracker', so I certainly knew what it was to be 'blessed with an angel'. My husband Andre and I both longed for a daughter and it took another five years before Sarah arrived in all her glory. At the time of Kristo's death, Sarah was just about to turn one. Kristo was 7, Jason was 13.

Letter to God

Why did I have to lose him,
Why did grief crush my heart,
Where were you
When my life was torn apart?

How could you turn away from me
When I was shaken to the core,
My roots and my foundations torn?
Did I still need to experience more?

~ Anne Pieterse

Chapter Two

"But let there be spaces in your togetherness and let the winds of the heavens dance between you. Love one another but make not a bond of love: let it rather be a moving sea between the shores of your souls."
~ Kahlil Gibran

GONE FOREVER

Kristo's body was never recovered, and his name was placed on the 'missing' list. The years of agony without closure were hard. I have since found my own closure and peace with Mother Earth, as it was an element of Mother Earth that swallowed our son.

I have made peace with Mother Earth and am at one with her now. Here is my story:

We had travelled eight hours to the coast as Andre, my husband, was attending a conference. We decided to book an apartment by the sea. I grew up at the sea, and it was my second home. My eldest brother's son, Neil, who was also seven at the time, joined us for a few days. He happened to live close to where we would be staying and stayed over for the night. Early the next morning we packed a bag and after breakfast and went down to the beach.

Lost

It was early one morning
The day had broken
Sweating from the humidity of the heat
The children wanted to play.

We followed the path to the beach
Found a grassy spot near the top
Unpacked the towels and spades
And off they hopped.

I went down to the water's edge
To watch the boys play
Feet splashing through the water
This would be an endless day.

One wave broke at the water's edge
And knocked them off their feet
Then pulled them deeper
And way out of reach.

I watched the waves, helpless,
Babe in arm, I couldn't help
I froze
A brave man rushed into the sea
He returned with one.

~ Anne Pieterse

Kristo's life was taken so unexpectedly: one minute he was having fun with his cousin and the next they were both sucked out to sea by a 'rip tide'. His body was never recovered.

At this time of grief you are praying as hard as you can; you are talking to God and 'not getting any answers', 'your heart ripped open by the pain' as you have lost a precious child unexpectedly. Nothing can ease the pain, nothing and no one. Breathing is difficult, it is as though you are breathing without receiving any air. It's worse than breathing through a straw. It's as though an elephant is sitting on your chest.

Feelings:

- No medication can numb the pain we feel.
- Something within us has died, and it is very hard to carry on. Many of us don't want to.
- We are 'frozen' with anxiety and find it hard to breathe.
- Simply putting one foot in front of the other is difficult.
- You are finding it difficult to eat and swallow. Try drinking more nourishing drinks. Try some soup and soft foods.
- There is no meaning at this stage. What I did find useful one day, is that we were at a shopping centre and they had shop which printed out family names and the meanings. We found this useful and took this with us to the Service to go alongside his enlarged Photo.
- Logic and emotions don't go together. Make no rash decisions at this stage.

Chapter Three

"And ever has it been known that love knows not its own depth until the hour of separation"

~ Kahlil Gibran

SHOCK

It wasn't long—maybe 20 minutes—before word of what had happened became public. I walked up to the Lifeguard Station with Neil and asked them for a 'tablet'. They gave me a paracetamol. I had more than a headache: I was numb, I was in shock and disbelief. I couldn't believe what was happening. It felt like a dream.

Neil was in shock too and kept crying out 'my cousin, my cousin'and pointed to the sea. It was like being in a trance. We both couldn't believe what had happened. Kristo was swept out so fast: with Neil one moment, and gone the next. Neil asked and then too realised, after very little explanation, that Kristo was not coming back. Complete realisation of the situation, meanwhile, began to dawn on me at the same time. It was like a dream.

After a short while standing staring at the ocean, I think I was waiting for Kristo to walk out of the sea as if nothing happened. I was met by a plain clothes detective who had heard what had happened. He was assigned to the case, and did not leave us for the next 12 hours.

My husband had now arrived in shock. We packed up our things and headed back to the holiday apartment, detective in tow.

Although he did give us some space to talk, everything was written down and noted.

I had done nothing wrong, but I think he was part of the team co-ordinating everything; the beach patrol, search, etc. My memories of him were good and he needed to explain quite a few things to us regarding the 'search and recovery' and which mortuary our son's body would be taken if it were to be recovered or washed up.

He was more of a 'father' figure to me and I felt comforted despite all the questions asked. We needed to start our own airborne sea search. The air search we would have to pay for ourselves. I couldn't believe what I was hearing.

My brother was trained as a 'navy diver' and I began to realise that our only help would be through him. I had the terrible task of asking him if he would co-ordinate the sea rescue from above. He obliged, and happened to have a friend with a microlight whom he would ask to assist. All we needed to do was pay for the two-stroke oil the microlight used. Plan on—this went ahead the next day.

I begged him look for our son as if he was looking for his own. I know this was a tall order for him. He was in shock too and had to drop everything he was doing and still cope with this. He told me in no uncertain terms that he was not looking for our son, he was looking for the body. He wanted to know what colour swimming costume he was wearing so they knew what colour may catch their eyes. It was blue and aquamarine, the Speedo type. I immediately started to blame myself for not buying the brighter 'neon orange' costume that was next to the one we eventually did buy. This was the costume Kristo wanted, he chose the colour. I had to live with that.

The 'search and recovery' lasted the next few days. It later diminished to beach patrols, and dissipated after about 8 days. After about eight days, we now needed to start thinking of some kind of a 'remembrance service' for our darling son. We had a Memorial Service fourteen days later. It was heartbreaking.

Words of Wisdom

- There are so many ifs, if onlys and what ifs? . . . You need to stop these as soon as you can as they will drive you mad.

- You don't know what loss is, but day by day it gradually sinks in that our loved one is not coming back. Nothing can ease the pain, nothing.

Chapter Four

"Once a word leaves your mouth, you cannot chase it back even with the swiftest horse."

~ Chinese Proverb

THE INSENSITIVE THINGS PEOPLE SAY:

When a mother loses her child it is the closest thing to being insane that we ever will be. Not to say that the other family members are not hurting. We know they hurt too. Mother's have carried the child, some have given birth and most of all we are the ones who nurture our children. Unless you have lost a child you will never know what we are going and live through. Hence I have made a list of the *insensitive* things people say to us.

The things people say that hurt:

- It was his time.
- It's your fault. To those parent's who were last with the child. The blame.
- Maybe it was meant to be. Perhaps there was something wrong with the child. It's nature's way. (miscarriage or stillbirth deaths). How can we be sure for certain?
- You can always try again.
- I know how you feel. – Only you know how you feel, nobody else.

- I feel your pain.
- Why are you so down today?
- God doesn't give you a load more than you can handle.
- He/she is in a better place now. What child of yours would you have sacrificed??
- It will get better. What will get better, my grief, my life, what?
- You are lucky you still have other children.
- It could have been worse.
- You'll get over it. When will that be?
- You can have another child can't you? Why would I want a replacement, nothing will replace the child I have lost.
- When are you going back to work?
- You'll be fine tomorrow.
- Don't ask us if we are over it. We will *never* get over it.
- The sins of the father are carried down 5 generations – What a Minister told me four weeks after losing Kristo! This is just what I didn't need to hear. That sounded like a curse! Did my God practice Witchcraft or the Occult? I have never heard something so infuriating in all my life. I am not going to ask for the forgiveness of my father's sins or his generations, how would I even know what they were? They were responsible for their own actions not me.

*"I had touched Hell already and needed to turn
to Spirituality to touch Heaven."*

– Anne Pieterse

Special things that help when you don't know what to do or say to those in grief:

- *Write a card, send a letter* – I think in this modern day of all our technology an email would not be personal and I would prefer to send a handwritten letter or card. Some poetry that was sent to me in cards I found helpful. If you are miles away from a person then you would maybe find an email or ecard more appropriate.
- *Listen* – one of the greatest things to do is just listen, whether it is with them or over the phone.
- *Comfort* – Hugs are always well appreciated without words, unless you can find the right ones. I always battle to find the right words myself, there are few, a hug is worth 1000 words.
- *Support* – Our greatest need at this time is support, love and companionship. There are so many things that we all need to

sort out and arrange and support helps enormously. Between all the emotions that we are experiencing, we may still have to think logically as we have things we need to sort out.

- *Gifts* – offerings of light meals to the family are always welcome. There is no time to think of cooking or looking after oneself. This is a very kind gesture, arriving at the house with something, however small it may be. There may be other children hurting and needing attention and they will always welcome food.
- *Meals*—If you are unable to afford to offer a meal, then maybe you would like to offer to cook a meal at their home for them. A lighter meal or soup is easier to digest and it can also be difficult to swallow at this time.
- *Flowers* – most definitely do brighten up some very somber days and are always welcome. Some flowers from your garden are also most welcome.
- *Kitchen*—It is very hard for a mother or husband to go into the kitchen and cook, because the hub of the family is normally in and around the kitchen. The one you are used to nurturing is no longer with you. It took me ages to cook a 'family meal' again.
- *Remembering*—Please do mention the child's name, the child is still with them and will always be a part of us. It's not someone we forget or can ever forget. It's quite usual to talk about the child. Using their name acknowledges them.
- *Music* – In early grief can be very distressing as you are reminded of the songs you and your loved one may have shared or liked. There are many triggers and music is one of them and one you can't control if you are in a shopping centre or shop.

We are constantly reminded of our loss.

Chapter Five

"He who blames others has a long way to go on his journey.
He who blames himself is halfway there.
He who blames no one has arrived"

~ Chinese proverb

BETRAYAL

On arriving home three weeks later, my 'late' alcoholic mother-in-law, told me that 'I couldn't have been watching my son otherwise he wouldn't have drowned'. She went on to tell me that when she took her children to the beach when they were young, she used to tie a rope around their waist! My husband sided with her immediately. He was in his own grief and experiencing his own anger and pain and was in a blaming frame of mind. I questioned whether if I had heard her correctly. I had. I was devastated to my very core. Not only had we lost our beautiful son, but I was been blamed for this, too. How cruel people (and this was my family) can be at a time of sorrow. My body was almost paralysed with the pain, fear, rejection, guilt and betrayal. The reality of this was that I was blinded like a fool into believing them. I swallowed their emotional poison. This was a lesson I would pay dearly for and would nearly cost me my own life. I forgave my husband on a level after a long time and much family counselling, but the pain my mother-in-law had inflicted on me lingered on. She was convinced that I was a bad mother and that I hadn't watched my son. She never took her words back. It was years later,

28

when trying to come to terms with this blame (and it's a place I still visit), that I made some sense of the whole suggestion.

If I wasn't watching the boys, both seven-years-old at the time, then how did we get Neil out alive? The children were playing together on the sand, ankle deep in water, bathing between the beacons. One moment there was a wave, they lost their balance and were churned upside down, and finally a rip tide swept them out to sea. I have now made peace with this, but it infuriates me how insensitive some people can be and how your own family can betray you when you need them most.

I took her words personally and internalised my pain. I was physically bleeding—hemorrhaging—inside, which is very symbolic of the pain, shock and loss I was experiencing. I would go to a specialist to have the blood that had accumulated under the skin at the base of my neck aspirated. My womb would weep for months to come. It was my body's natural response to emotional abandonment and the deep-seated toxic shame and hurt that goes with it. My life force was leaving me. My chest was crushed, and felt as if it had been vacuum-sealed. It was hard to breathe. My breathing and heart-rate wouldn't slow down. I was physically strangled and lost my voice over and over again. Grief had 'captured me and held me to ransom'. It was torturing me and it wouldn't let me go.

Thief in the Night
Grief attacks your mind, body and soul
Holds them to ransom
And then lets them go again.
Then just as you've turned away
Without any warning,
Returns to capture you.

~ Anne Pieterse

The support system I thought I had simply crumbled beneath my feet. Judging is itself a cruel and dangerous thing to do. Don't judge others and especially not in death, or grief. My God is not a cruel God, my God doesn't judge; why was God letting me go through all this pain? No one was protecting me, I felt naked and exposed; I only had myself to rely on. I was a mother in grief. I felt an overwhelming sense of failure; I had failed, failed to protect my son, failed to save his life, failed to recover his body and failed myself and my family. I was swamped in my own guilt. Basically, I had given up and wanted to die.

A few months later, at a 'Compassionate Friends Meeting', our facilitator read one of the most beautiful poems I have ever heard. This poem challenged and empowered me and gave me courage and strength to transform my life. It went like this:

The Invitation

by: Oriah

It doesn't interest me what you do for a living.
I want to know what you ache for
and if you dare to dream of meeting your heart's longing.

It doesn't interest me how old you are.
I want to know if you will risk looking like a fool
for love
for your dream
for the adventure of being alive.

It doesn't interest me what planets are squaring your moon . . .
I want to know if you have touched the centre of your own sorrow
if you have been opened by life's betrayals
or have become shrivelled and closed
from fear of further pain.

I want to know if you can sit with pain
mine or your own
without moving to hide it
or fade it
or fix it.

I want to know if you can be with joy
mine or your own
if you can dance with wildness
and let the ecstasy fill you to the tips of your fingers and toes
without cautioning us
to be careful
to be realistic
to remember the limitations of being human.

It doesn't interest me if the story you are telling me
is true.
I want to know if you can
disappoint another
to be true to yourself.
If you can bear the accusation of betrayal
and not betray your own soul.

WHAT IF I WHISPERED YOUR NAME?

If you can be faithless
and therefore trustworthy.

I want to know if you can see Beauty
even when it is not pretty
every day.
And if you can source your own life
from its presence.

I want to know if you can live with failure
yours and mine
and still stand on the edge of the lake
and shout to the silver of the full moon,
"Yes."

It doesn't interest me
to know where you live or how much money you have.
I want to know if you can get up
after the night of grief and despair
weary and bruised to the bone
and do what needs to be done
to feed the children.

It doesn't interest me who you know
or how you came to be here.
I want to know if you will stand
in the centre of the fire
with me
and not shrink back.

It doesn't interest me where or what or with whom
you have studied.
I want to know what sustains you
from the inside
when all else falls away.

I want to know if you can be alone
with yourself
and if you truly like the company you keep
in the empty moments.

***

The group sat quietly for a few minutes. Nobody moved or said a word. There were many tears. I felt totally at ease and comforted by the fact that someone out there knew what the centre of grief felt like, somebody who had touched their own sorrow. The poem touched me deeply and, more than that, it challenged me.

We tend to put up a barrier after the death of a loved one, a 'wall of grief' that no one can penetrate because we are so wounded.

I most certainly was touching my own sorrow at that very instant and could identify with becoming shriveled and closed from fear of further pain. I was right there, that moment, in that room. I can remember it so clearly, I remember the wisdom in the poem so clearly, a poem that 'touched' my sorrow and would transform my life!

We try to keep safe from any further pain because we have so much fear. In fact, I did not want to look, see, feel or be with anyone. I just wanted to be with myself and my pain. I am surprised I even heard what the facilitator was reading! I was looking at the floor!

I didn't mind being lonely by myself, and loved my own company. **But,** being alone in those 'empty moments', on your own path of grief, when you have touched your own sorrow, is a very, very lonely and painful place to be. You just have to trust yourself, embrace the pain and feel it; there is nothing else you can do. It is paralysing to feel this pain. If you don't feel it and you push it away, the pain comes back twofold and will keep coming back until you have dealt with it. Feel the pain, as hard as it is and stand up to your fears 'head on'. Try and find the strength and courage.

This poem was a turning point for me, something to work on and something to live for. Here was someone in all their humanness who appeared brave enough to touch their own sorrow and not move from it; they embraced it and found the courage to do this. Oriah was challenging me to stand in the fire with her and not shrink back. I felt a sense of belonging, a sense of purpose, something for which I could feel alive. I was empowered by words so simple and, I think more importantly for me, 'the challenge' that it presented. It was the ultimate challenge for me. The words in the poem made me reconsider my thoughts about facing the *fire* in front of me that I was terrified of, made me find the courage to acknowledge my own failures and sit with them, to still get up and do what needed to be done for the children and, more importantly, to be brave enough to touch my own sorrow and lastly to be able to sit at the edge of the lake and shout 'Yes' to the silver moon.

I love challenges; I go the whole way with them. I love being challenged. Nothing can be as difficult as touching your own sorrow and surviving. The worst grief in life is supposed to be that of a parent who has lost a child or children.

I love challenging others too! No challenges can be worse than the one's I have already faced, or at least I certainly hope not!

My biggest challenge facing me at that very moment was that I was in my deepest depression and loss and had no idea how to get out nor did I have the courage to make the change.

Truths:

- During the group meetings at The Compassionate Friends, I was present and listening even if I thought I wasn't because I was not 'engaged' or interacting in the conversation. I was just there hoping for a miracle I guess.
- You can find the courage and strength even if it is only enough to get you through to the end of the day.
- The only way to go forward is to live and think only one moment and then one day at a time. It's enough; we can't cope with much more.
- There is no need to plan ahead, our plans for the future have been shattered anyway. Planning didn't work for me but created more anxiety.
- Don't think of tomorrow, it can wait. You need to take 'baby steps' and need to crawl before you can walk again.
- There may be many 'dark nights of the soul' and many more ahead where you will be faced with loneliness and desolation. You need to face these and understand that you are going through a process. This process takes time and patience.

Thoughts:

- Would our loved one who has passed on want to see us in all this pain?
- How do you think it would make them feel?
- What do you think they would like to see?
- What do you think they would like to see you doing right now?
- *Crying, being miserable, depressed and having no life at all? NO*
- Write down some feelings, work with them.

Trapped

Trapped in an abyss, with no sense of time
No purpose or direction
Groveling in the thick, choking fog,
Grief consumed my every breath,
My heart pounding, my energy draining.

A black slippery bottomless pit
Became my home,
I could not climb out, I had no strength,
Laying motionless, poisoned,
From all the stress and emotional pain.
I couldn't move.
Every inch of me ached.
I had lost my life.

I looked for answers, there were none,
I gazed to the light but I could not see.
Clutching onto nothingness in this hot, dark,
claustrophobic existence,
I needed to be rescued,
But only I could choose.
Was this going to be my destiny?
Look at what I had to lose.

Deep within my very being
Something urged me to get out
I was beginning to suffocate.
I had to make a choice.
My children needed me desperately,
I did not find the courage to stay.

~ Anne Pieterse

"When you gaze long into the abyss, the abyss also gazes into you"
—Friedrich Nietzsche (1844-1900)

Chapter Six

FINDING INTIMACY

"A friend is someone who walks in when the rest of the world walks out"
~ Unknown

Today, I met up with someone a bit younger than myself 'who has been through her own pain'. It was not the loss of a child, but grief and her own sorrow from a life-changing experience. The importance sharing these stories is that it allows you to feel and experience intimacy at a time of sorrow. We go through a grieving process and nobody can by-pass it. When I mentioned to her that I was 'writing a book' we shared a few brief moments of our personal experience. We somehow got onto the best part: 'betrayal'. She then started telling me about an event in her life 'which she didn't know was my story too'.

These are moments of unfathomable longing during grief and despair, something we have an unquenchable ache and craving for.

I felt the 'healing power of sharing' shining through and I trust you will too. Maybe it will be something you identify with or maybe something you have gone through yourself. I loved her story, we laughed together. I found myself in her story too. I was amazed she trusted me enough to tell me about 'her affair' and how she had also betrayed her husband and family at this time of longing. I didn't feel so alone. When you are betrayed during your grief, you may crave love and acceptance and a sense of belonging. I didn't share mine with her but did send her an

35

email that evening thanking her for being so honest in sharing, and told her about my 'affair' too. Sharing is important and it allows us to heal through your own personal stories. I am going to share my story with you now to show that when the one you love turns their back on you or betrays you, you may seek an alternative at that very moment as the longing is so intense—a longing for love, touch and acceptance. I am simply showing you what can happen and did happen to me and do not encourage this at all.

This is the story of when I felt I betrayed my family.

During my 'lost' stage, when I found myself in a 'bottomless pit of grief and depression', I was trapped. I was so trapped I had to 'run away' from my family. I was running from my pain, from my betrayal, from the pit I was in. I had to escape.

On a Friday evening, I would prepare the family dinner early, check if my children were alright and then leave home when my husband got back from work and check into a 'budget hotel'. I needed time away, I needed to hide. I could neither help myself nor my grief nor face my whole life with all this pain. I did this frequently. I was an emotional wreck: I was embarrassed by all the pain and felt ashamed, weak and had lost my self-worth. I could not accept nor face my pain.

This was a dysfunctional trait I had learnt. All I knew was to run away from problems. I couldn't face them. I didn't have the time nor had the 'privilege' of having a nervous breakdown nor did I want to go down that route. I still had a son of 13 with cystic fibrosis and a daughter of one to look after. Not forgetting my husband, with whom I was so annoyed at the time and whom I wanted to punish for being cruel with his words. I had to get a grip on my own reality and face my own fears. I didn't know how, did not have the tools to do this, but my therapist devised a plan and was trying to help me stop 'running away'. It took a while before she taught me 'coping strategies'. This 'coping' means without 'dissociating' (one of my favorite things to do, as this was another way of not facing my grief).

I too found love, not 'true love', but love. A very soft and gentle love. I had met someone during a workshop I had been on. I guess you can say we had an affair, an intimate love, a words-and-poetry affair. It was not a sexual affair—pretty close, though—but I had no energy for sex anyway and that was not what I wanted nor what I was looking for. I had an overwhelming desire to find this love and acceptance.

I had experienced the pain of my father having an affair and I was not going to let history repeat itself, although I was on the verge of doing so. I did not want my children to go through that pain too. But the acceptance from another being without being betrayed, being accepted for who you are, being comforted and listened to: this new love I found, it fed and soothed my body and soul, and it was exciting, nourishing and just what I needed at the time. I could feel my adrenaline pumping, too! This may have awoken my senses.

Some of the most famous public figures have affairs, and these affairs all seem to take place during a time of betrayal. There seems to be a very prominent thread here with betrayal and how we turn away to find love. It's not a good idea to judge this process of betrayal, but what I am trying to put across is the sharing of true stories of betrayal and what we do. This is the truth about what can happen, and not 'what went wrong' because I don't know anyone who did not enjoy their 'affair'. I certainly had no regrets.

At the time, my 'lover' was writing and publishing poetry on grief 'and I was listening day and night to it', mostly over the phone. We would read books, 'real life stories', and war stories and go through the pain and grief of them together. We would talk about grief, his and mine, for hours and days on end. We would play beautiful music and lie in each other's arms, caressing each other until we realized the consequences of the temptation of going any further.

At the end of our relationship he wrote a beautiful poem about me called 'The Dandelion'. One blow on a dandelion and it fragments into millions of pieces. That was me alright, swaying with the wind, fragmented, shattered and yet looking for something that would bring me together again, put me back into something more solid and turn me into a 'rose'. I identified so well with music and poetry, and loved it. It spoke straight to my heart and soul and nurtured me.

Thoughts:

Even through pain and betrayal, when life is not pretty every day, you can find comfort and solace. Don't be fooled in looking too far for it!

Chapter Seven

"You can tell the size of your God by looking at the size of your worry list. The longer your list, the smaller your God."

~ Unknown

IS THERE A GOD?

Has God been lost in the shuffle and the separation of our mind, body and soul that feels like it has been ripped out of us? I am talking about a relationship with God and not about religion at all.

Where is God?

Are you there when I knock?
Are you there when I call?
Why did you let this happen?
Is there a God after all?

~ Anne Pieterse

Be still, relax, close your eyes and go within for a few moments and ask yourself this one question:

"Where is God?"

WHAT IF I WHISPERED YOUR NAME? 39

There are endless questions and answers and sometimes we are looking too far for the answer.

"Help us to find God."

"No one can help you there."
"Why not?"
"For the same reason that no one can help the fish to find the ocean."
~ Unknown

The highest spirituality says there is no separation between the creator and his creation.

Here are some more Unknown Author quotes I have found to ponder on:

- Without clouds . . . there can be no rain.
- God hides things by putting them all around us.
- God often visits us . . . but most of the time we are not at home.

  Happy moments . . . Praise God
  Difficult moments . . . Seek God
  Quiet moments . . . Worship God
  Painful moments . . . Trust God
  Every moment . . . Thank God

- Faith can move mountains.
- When you have learned how to decide with God, all decisions become easy and right as breathing.
- To forget troubles—remember God.
- Loneliness comes when I forget that God is my supreme companion.
- When the world becomes like a wild storm . . . the most beautiful shelter is God.
- Fear is simply faith in the dark forces . . . Stay in the Light
- The fruits that the spirit produce are: love, joy, peace, patience, kindness, goodness, faithfulness, gentleness and self-control.

  Divine Light . . . Within me . . . As me . . . Through me
  Blesses and multiplies
  All that I am . . . All that I have . . . and All that I circulate.

Sorrow looks back
Worry looks around
Faith looks up

- Faith is believing that the universe is on our side, and the universe knows what it's doing.

Chapter Eight

"Anyone who says sunshine brings happiness has never danced in the rain."
~ *Unknown*

HOPE—SPIRITUAL ALCHEMY

I felt the need to contact 'Oriah', and so I did. We communicated: I felt more alive and this also brought her writing alive! This was a real human being, someone with feelings, who had written this, someone who had touched their own sorrow.

One week later, I booked into a 'Native American Workshop' held by Michael Owen. Michael is a clinical psychologist and Jungian psychotherapist who has travelled widely and apprenticed himself for many years with inter-tribal elders in indigenous medicine. A close friend of mine, Therese, was organizing this event and she thought it would be wonderful if I came along. She had absolutely no idea about where I was in my grief and had no idea what Oriah's poem meant to me. I had never spoken to her about it, ever.

I sat in the circle in the workshop and the introductions started. Michael first introduced himself, who he was and where he had studied. This was not important to me. Then Therese went on to say that he used to co-teach with Oriah and had now moved to New Zealand. I thought WOW! Then 'The Invitation' by Oriah, got read out again. Well, I think I was shell-shocked. When it came to introducing myself, I didn't say much, I forgot everything, who I was, why I was there. I now know why

41

I was there, to experience spiritual alchemy at its peak and to feel alive! This moment would be the closest I would get to Oriah.

I told Therese the impact all this was having on me in a matter of one week! She was not very fazed by my excitement at all (she is a very grounded person). That evening she handed me a book, 'a fable', to read. I was in 'spiritual heaven'. I was experiencing the alchemy. She was the 'alchemist' who put this all together and showed me the way by pointing me in the right direction that day. She was enjoying the chemistry and was teaching me how to symbolically marry things up. Easy $1 + 1 = \ldots$ I had the $1 + 1$ but never found the beauty and the mystery unfolded in the answer. It's a lovely feeling to guide people to this process of transformation and then watch as something comes alive and you can make total sense of it. It's a way to manifest physical and spiritual abundance in your life.

Coincidences don't happen, there are no such things. Where I was at that place at that time was going to happen. This was **life** I was experiencing, and the spiritual alchemy of it. I was now 'living a dream', appreciating and feeling the power of such a beautiful experience, an experience of how anyone can become an alchemist in your own life, perhaps without them even being aware of it. If you are living consciously and 'in the moment' you will see the alchemy and its beauty and find the gold.

I immediately started picking up the pieces of my life, started to find direction and meaning in everything around me. Life got more interesting and more meaningful. Living 'consciously' was this brand new world for me. Engaging and being conscious takes a lot of energy and hard work. You are like a 'sieve', and everything that goes through or past you gets filtered, but you will reap the benefits of the hard work.

Wow! Now everything was now starting to make sense. I had something to live for.

I could gradually start making sense of life and give a meaning to events. I started going through a type of spiritual madness. I read like crazy, I listened to teachings, I was empowered. My new life was beginning to feel more interesting.

I was going to heal, and this set the spiritual foundation for my healing process to begin. Nothing was going to stop me.

Chapter Nine

"Believe in yourself and all that you are. Know that there is something inside you that is greater than any obstacle."

~ Unknown

FINDING DIRECTION THROUGH SYMBOLISM

What I had found from the teachings was something as simple as A B C (building blocks to re-build my life); finding direction, meaning and symbolism in life's little things, simple things. I fully believe that there are no coincidences in life, absolutely none. There is a reason for every single event. You need to look out for the magic in things. You need to be aware what is going on. People cross our path for a reason. Do we try and find the purpose in these events?

Finding reason and meaning to be alive, finding the courage to embrace pain, trying to make sense of it, (although extremely difficult at the time) living with meaning and working with my dreams every day gave me comfort, showed me where I was on my path and became a fascinating adventure. . . I didn't have to pay for or spend a lot of money on any of this. I had everything I came to earth with. We are all equipped with our own life-force, our own inner compass and own intuition: we know everything; we just need to awaken ourselves to use it and find our own answers. We need to go within and look for our own answers.

I needed something; I needed the very basics for survival.

In total honesty, here I was 'the victim' and lost. There was just 'me' in this whole world and I was in enormous pain. That's all I knew.

Everything within me died. I felt naked, I felt stripped to the bone, I was exposed, frightened and I was in a very vulnerable place—the 'freezing arctic winter of my grief'.

I was just a person with a brain that didn't want to function, a soul that had given up and a body that couldn't move. There was nothing left of me. I was losing weight. I had nearly lost my life force.

I couldn't think for myself, had completely lost my voice and faced a battle to regain my sight. I couldn't see because I didn't want to see!

I couldn't feel, I was numb to just about everyone and everything.

I had to start again. This was my only way and my saving grace.

I had found a very simple and basic survival guide that helped me heal and become the person I am today, the person who can now face any challenge, any time, head-on or with stealth.

I desperately needed direction, so I turned to the simple basics of our universe.

I discovered the Medicine Wheel, a symbol of Native American psychology, and what it represents.

I looked for direction because my own internal compass was broken, I found it, and that's the very point at which I started. This is the journey I needed to go on to find my own path.

Within the Medicine Wheel are the Four Cardinal Directions and the Four Sacred Colors.

North, South, East, West . . . simple.

I bought a compass and found true north, south, east and west. I made my own Medicine Wheel from small rocks I had collected. Every day I watched the sun rise in the east and set in the west. Day after day, I noticed the soft pink colors absorbing and embracing the beauty of the universe, watching some of the most incredible sunrises and sunsets. Watching the clouds go by the different formations, feeling the wind on my skin finding my own breath and rhythm. Walking and feeling the soft grass under my feet. Just being alive—experiencing the beauty of Mother Nature!

For weeks that's all I did. Absorbed Mother Nature—the beauty, the flowers; took time to smell them. I always looked for the tiniest little flower (those ones between the grass with little yellow, white or purple petals) and admired their beauty.

The circle in the Medicine Wheel represents the Circle of Life, and in the centre of the circle is the Eternal Fire.

I then realised that much in nature was round. The sun, the sky, the earth, the planets, the stars and the moon. I looked for the beauty in them. I found the beauty.

I experienced every breath that passed my lips, felt the warm wind tingling on my arms, sat and enjoyed the warm rain that fell sideways on my face. I experienced nature to its fullest. I listened to the wind, the storms and the lightning. I particularly dislike storms and the cold and, most certainly, an angry sea. It is a mother's instinct to wrap your child up and keep them safe and warm. That's what you want to do. I have heard that other mothers experience the same thing too, so I didn't feel alone or crazy.

I had lost my son but kept experiencing the instinct. I still do today, but on a much less intense level. It's a very strong instinct and, after much challenging of myself, my wisdom and knowledge reassure me he's okay.

I am now at one with the universe, the sea, the sky, the blueness of it, the breath and heartbeat of Mother Nature which feeds and nourishes me; ONE.

Both women and the moon have a 28-day cycle. Just as the moon goes through different phases, ranging from full to new moon, visible to invisible.

I also discovered the healing power of music. Music therapy definitely had a profound effect on my healing and helped to turn me around. I started to listen to more music, and to make music a part of my life and the healing process. I found a song for every grieving stage and even listened to 'Knocking on Heaven's Door'. The lyrics were so true.

> *"I knocked on heaven's door, it did not open, the time was not right for me."*
>
> **~ Anne Pieterse**

A few years later, I knew I had to be physically present in this world if I wanted to carry on. I had to live consciously and I chose to. I was terrified, as the state of 'consciousness' takes an enormous amount of energy and hard work. It is endless. But 'now is the only time there is', so I needed to live consciously in 'the moment'. Conscious living has been the saving grace for my transformation.

Early one morning, as I awoke, I felt a weight had been lifted off me. I felt transformed. I was light my head was clear, my breathing was easier. It was a beautiful summer's day. The liquid rays of the sun were streaming into my bedroom. I jumped out of bed, ripped open my bedroom curtains and decided, and there was no going back. I said goodbye to depression and 'hello' to being alive. I have never looked back. My attitude had shifted, it was a 'quantum leap' for me. I started getting my direction back from nature.

Chapter Ten

MY 5 SEASONS OF GRIEF

"As the garden grows, so does the gardener"
– Unknown

I then watched the changes of the seasons very carefully. There is a common thread that runs through grief, which symbolically resembles the Four Seasons: Winter, Spring, Summer, Fall. I have also experienced a very cold and icy Arctic Winter, when I was in a very deep depression that was so difficult to emerge from, and so I have added another season. So I am calling this 'My 5 Seasons of Grief' just to be creative!

Grief shares a symbolic unity with the seasons of Mother Earth. It is here that we can merge with this beauty, which will in turn allow us to identify which season of grief we are in and enlighten us to the gifts we share together. She helps us awaken our senses and invites us to experience her beauty, the greatness, the power and connection we have with her.

I have always dreamed of being a painter, that's what I would like to do for a day job! I visualise in my mind picking up a wide paintbrush and painting on a clean white canvas. Painting and drawing is something I have not mastered. One of my many weaknesses! I sit in the lounge early on a Saturday and watch a television program on painting. The calm and serene painter explaining what picture he is going to paint today, the colour and canvas he is going to use before he paints a beautiful picturesque landscape.

He first paints the blue background of the sky, followed by the white freedom of the fluffy clouds as they dance across the sky, then moves down to the base of the picture to paint the water and rocks. He then changes colours and uses a stipple brush to start on the green leaves to make a tree. Then carefully he whispered in the twigs and strong branches in tones of brown and moves down to steady the trunk of the tree in the earth. He then explains how he is going to add some depth and dimension into the picture by shading in the pictures and making shadows. He lets the shadows of the tree fall in a certain way according to the direction of the sun and shows how the light influences the silver shadows as they fall sideways on to the lake.

I have decided to paint a picture for you so you too can visualize the colors of grief in your mind's eye. This is the creative expression I use and am going to share with you so that it gives you the tools to creatively paint your own inner landscape, a place you can visit time and again. You will be able to change your canvas and pictures using your own creative pallet of colors to feel and experience the magic. This will enable you to use your grief creatively and the expression and energy from it in a nurturing way

It is important to allow ourselves to feel these emotions so that we can move through the different stages of our grieving process.

Arctic Winter

If you are experiencing an Arctic Winter, this could be at the very beginning of your grief or even later on.

This is when grief captured me and held me to ransom. Did I want to live or die? I wanted to die, as I felt there was nothing more to live for. I wanted to die pining for the one I had lost. I never thought of an overdose, although many people at this stage think of something drastic to do. Life does not feel worth living at all.

The Arctic Winter was one of the most painful experiences during grief. You are helpless. Nothing you tell anyone is going to make any difference, and I was not going to listen to anyone either. It's a very stubborn time, during which you are coming to terms with what has happened, with how your life and dreams have been shattered, and absolutely nothing matters when you are here.

This is a very icy cold place, which you have not experienced before. You have isolated yourself, the wind is icy, you can't keep warm, your breathing is erratic and frightening and it feels like your every breath is squeezed out of you. Much like when you put food in a packet to and start 'vacuum sealing' it, your breath is sucked away and you try to catch your next breath. I was consumed by panic attacks which left me terrified and drained any energy I had left to survive on.

This is a very frightening place to be, where you need help although you think you don't. You will need the help of a professional grief counsellor or the help of The Compassionate Friends support group. Even if you don't talk and tell your story, you can still share one or two feelings. Make yourself, or maybe someone you know of in this frightening and scary place, phone the group and a counsellor will phone your loved one. A doctor is not going to help you get through this stage; they can only numb the pain with drugs. You can still go and be part of a group of other bereaved parents/families who are in exactly the same situation you may be in now. Pick up the phone—please. Do something for yourself or for your loved one or friend. Just do it. I have seen what happens to those who don't choose this route. Please make the right choice, there are many survivors of grief out there and I am just one of them (one drop in the ocean) sharing my story with you.

It may be important that you go alone to these meetings without your partner or family member as you will be able to express yourself better. I found it easier alone because I made friends when I was there.

You will need to get through birthdays, anniversary dates, triggers, the list goes on and on. There is help waiting right now for you. Help yourself.

Winter

You could be experiencing the **winter** of your grief. This could be when you begin to feel your entire life weighing heavily upon you. You may hibernate, just like the animals who are cold, and some of them not strong enough to brace themselves through the winter. Know that if you don't protect and look after yourself, keep yourself warm and well fed, you too will get sick or die. You may feel the need to keep warm and protected in something that would caress your skin with its fluffy, gentle, warm touch. The seeds and fruit you have gathered in the autumn will nourish and feed you through the winter.

This winter could have longer nights, which may be cold, grey, dark, lifeless, slippery, wet and frozen with stark scenery. The starkness of winter also reveals more clearly our wounded self and our tendency to project our fear, hopelessness or despair onto others.

This could leave the tall trees bare without leaves, the trunk exposed and without protection. Your sap may be drained too and you may feel that this will never rise again. Keep yourself very warm and comfortable, extra warm really. We feel the cold when we grieve and need to look after ourselves.

Just as our seasons of grief change, the winter will end and we will carry on just like the seasons.

The world refused to stop and wait for me so that I could jump off! I was orbiting the earth.

(A bit like a merry-go-round, that keeps spinning and is difficult to jump off when you want to).

The rate I had slowed down to could not keep up with the demands of the world—it was no longer serving me. I had to finally give in to accept the feelings and emotions grief had brought on me and move forward.

Spring will come! Wait patiently, you too will see Spring.

Spring

In the **Spring** of your grief, watch as your sap starts rising towards the warming sun. You will notice the gentle calls of the birds early in the morning, returning to nest. It's time to start renewing, gardening and renovating our homes, taking part in more outdoor activities and reconnecting with nature. It's time to clear out, 'spring clean', the clutter and the feelings of hurt and pain, the unnecessary burdens that are holding us back and that are no longer serving us.

We need to make space, get rid of the 'cobwebs', and rake our surface clear so that the sweet buds of spring can start shooting and transforming us into blossoming flowers which will color and fragrance our hearts and minds. Just like love, a fragile flower opening to the warmth of spring. Bulbs will start shooting up towards the light and there will be buds of new beginnings and ideas. Smell the freshly ploughed soil as the farmers plough their land. You need to paint your world, what you see on the outside and relate to your grief inside knowing that the warmth of summer will be coming and the grass underneath your feet will start re-nourishing and shooting after the grueling winter. *We need to trim the grass now to encourage new growth and stronger roots !*

When weeding, the best way to make sure you are removing a weed and not a valuable plant is to pull on it.
If it comes out of the ground easily, it is a valuable plant.
—Unknown

Summer

In the **Summer** of your grief, visualise your own picture of what summer feels, looks and smells like. You could start with a canvas of a blue cloudless sky, and then fill the sky with rainbows. Look at the colors, remember the promise the rainbow brings. You will feel the warm touch of the sun healing your body. Let it warm you up from the core, from the sorrow and pain, until you feel renewed and refreshed. Listen to the gentle music as the rain begins singing its songs and dancing on the ground. Smell the raindrops as they fall on a sandy road. Butterflies drink the sweet nectar from the newly opened flowers, showing us new life from the old. The reproductive organs of the flowers are now ripened, opened and waiting. The colors and the scent from the flowers, now full of nectar, attract and seduce the honey bee and the stigma waits in all its beauty to be pollinated.

Hear the cry of the eagles overhead with their outstretched wings floating on the thermals. Feel the freedom, feel summer, you are warm you are safe, you can let go. Smile. Enjoy the smell of fresh mown grass, the sweet scent of the roses. Be happy and feel loved. Appreciate what you have, even if it is small, from the 'free' gifts Mother Earth has to offer: the petals, the flowers, the feathers and the fruits. Open your heart to love and feel ripened and content, even if lasts for 'only a moment'. It's a time of trust and acceptance, knowing that 'summer' will come again. Feel it, be it.

Preparing for Fall / Autumn

Then **Autumn / Fall** starts, and the leaves begin to float down, lining the streets. Catch the cold crisp wind as it carries the leaves away. Each leaf sways, rushing against the many leaves on the floor, cascading into one another. The leaves start to move as if by some divine intervention, as if they were ready to travel wherever the wind blows. The last leaf falls off a tree, making it more barren then it was before. As it falls to the ground it is lifted up by a gust of wind. It floats further away into the distance, and it falls to the ground quietly. It is lost in the millions of orange, brown, and yellow; laying lifeless, turning brittle.

Autumn is a time full of moods and emotions and we too can start shedding some pain, guilts and emotions that have been burdening us so that we too can 'lighten' ourselves and prepare for the winter as the cycle of grief and its seasons continue.

My favorite autumn tree is the Japanese Maple. Watch as the different colors of red, orange and amber fade as the sap diminishes in the tree. The colors of the tree, which were once hidden beneath the green leaves, can now be seen and will be soon be fully exposed. This is nature's way of protecting the tree during the winter months. In the winter, trees get very little water through the roots. This way the tree can conserve water and stay alive. Fruits and nuts are harvested, the days become shorter, and animals start preparing for the winter as the days get cooler. Many changes occur during autumn.

Learning from the Squirrel and Preparing for Winter:

Squirrels have the ability to solve puzzles, are very resourceful and can change direction quickly. They store food for the future and can plan ahead. They balance giving and receiving and rest during times of stasis and avoid the danger of climbing higher. As the squirrels prepare for winter, they only gather what they require.

The teaching in this shows us the importance of letting go and getting rid of clutter, negative beliefs, emotions to make room for new things to come. The squirrel teaches us to lighten our load mentally, physically and emotionally.

Chapter Eleven

CHANGING TIDES

Anger

"Holding on to anger is like grasping a hot coal with the intent of throwing it at someone else; you are the one who gets burned."
~ *Buddha*

I have observed many parents in grief, and only a few have been angry and vengeful, for example if their child's death was perhaps caused by another. I have seen them go to extreme odds to get even with the other as they act out their anger and revenge. This anger takes so much energy and gradually eats you from the inside. They either want justice done or want to do it themselves. This is very dangerous, and although I could understand the circumstance, I could see no reason for their vindictiveness. This would not bring their loved one back at all. It's was like an ongoing war.

Verbal anger is a way of passing psychic pain on to others. It's a way of making others pay for your emotional deficits. Anger can become destructive, and this is when you may need professional help.

Anger can be used positively when dealing with grief and change if it is used properly without harming anyone. It is powerful and you can channel your anger constructively by using your creativity. Could it be holding you back from accepting the death of your loved one? It is

53

common for us to be angry at our loved one we have lost for leaving us because we can feel deserted or abandoned.

For me as the parent who was last with my child before he died, I felt enormous guilt. I am sure many others will identify with this too if they were in the same situation because we may have been the last responsible parent or person with the child. I wonder how many parents or others feel this guilt if they were with the child in these last moments? I blamed myself of course, I internalised my own anger inwards and for good measure added the blame on from my mother in law and to top it off finally the last words from the minister (see Chapter 4). My anger turned into deep depression. This is when I experienced the 'Arctic Winter of my Grief'.

I have always been a very introverted person who doesn't speak out. I began socially isolating myself; I didn't want to see anyone. I mean anyone. Because I couldn't face no one (or probably couldn't face anymore blame) because I thought everyone was judging me. I thought it was better just to have myself for company, although I didn't like myself at the time either. I couldn't sleep, had frightening panic attacks, couldn't go out because I didn't know when a panic attack would happen, I was in a total mess and just terrified of life and people. I was so scared of the depth of grief and internalised anger I found myself in, and decided to write the poem 'Trapped' more recently. I did this to honestly share and reflect my own experience so that others too can identify one of the dangerous places we could face in our grief. I can now see how far I have moved on from this 'Arctic Winter' I once experienced.

It was at the beginning stages of my 'Arctic Winter' that I phoned for help and called 'The Compassionate Friends'. They gave me the affirmation which is their credo that 'I Need Not Walk Alone'. I was able to later on able to verbalise my own guilt feelings and sharing this enormous guilt I eased the burden I was carrying. I don't think this guilt will ever completely go away. It lessens.

I have heard and am very aware that that if we bottle up our anger, this can cause many illnesses, including cancer.

Changing Attitudes

Forgiveness

"They may not deserve forgiveness, but I do"

~ *Unknown*

Forgiveness is a choice and up to us to make. 'For-I-give' frees the body to heal, frees your mind to be more constructive. You break the hold. For-I-give myself permission to accept the things I cannot change, give myself permission to grieve 'my way', permission to be kind to myself each day and give myself permission to forgive those who have hurt me because I deserve to be happy. Forgiving others and reclaiming your power and sending them in your mind's eye for recycling releases us immediately from the powerful hold they have over us that weighs us down.

Being able to make this conscious choice gives us a feeling of control over our emotions, over our situation, and in some cases over the outcome. When we forget that we have a choice, we leave ourselves open to feeling trapped, which in some cases may lead to depression.

- Forgiveness is what will free ourselves from the emotional and physical drain of anger and contribute to lifting and easing depression.

Forgiveness offers us a gift of freedom and frees us from the emotional hell. We first need to forgive ourselves and others so that we can be open to receiving and being compassionate toward others.

Letting go of hurt, pain, helplessness and anger is a step forward in healing. Forgiving will help us to release unwanted hurts and grudges from the past and opens our hearts to love, peace and happiness.

Forgiveness does not necessarily mean a reconciling with the one who hurt you, but it means finding peace and being at peace. Something we all deserve.

Practicing forgiveness, *including forgiving oneself for any regrets we harbor* is a positive step in helping yourself. We will begin to feel better more often, have improved sleep, experience more positive thoughts and emotions have happier healthier relationships and have a higher level of energy.

Acceptance of pain / Resolution

"When a parent dies, you lose your past; when a child dies,
you lose your future"

~ Unknown

We cannot change what has happened. Nothing can bring our loved one back, nothing. We need to accept this pain, we need to feel and experience it. Then, when it is no longer serving us, we need to let it go and accept what has happened, whether we want to or not. It's happened and there is nothing we can do to change what has happened. Of course this is going to take time but we also need to be kind to yourself and feel the benefits of acceptance.

We need to accept that we can continue forward with our lives and that we are allowed to feel pleasure, that we can have fun, laugh and go on holidays without feeling guilty. If we refuse to accept things, we will get stuck in the process of grief itself and it will become toxic. Through acceptance, we can move on. Acceptance brings us inner peace and tranquility.

There is no quick fix answer to how long this takes: it's a process, too. I can't even give you an answer on how long it took me, but long, I guess.

Gratefulness

"Gratitude is the best attitude"

~ Unknown

Gratitude increases abundance. Even if you have very little in life to be grateful for, notice what you have and appreciate it. Try and find between one to three things a day to be grateful for. Practicing gratitude daily can increase your happiness and attitude. It can also improve your mood, increase your level of alertness and improve your ability to maintain healthy relationships. Many people keep a gratitude journal, as they find it very beneficial and they begin to feeling more positive about their lives. Gratitude keeps us grounded, lifts our spirits, changes negative attitudes into being more positive and has positive health effects.

Smile

"Today, give a stranger one of your smiles. It might be the only sunshine he sees all day."

~ *Unknown*

When you smile at someone else, they smile and you are causing physiological changes within their bodies. Smiling has many therapeutic effects and health benefits. Smiling increases positivity, boosts the immune system, lowers blood pressure, reduces stress levels and changes other people's perception of you.

Affirmation

I deserve to be,
I want to be,
I can be,
I will be,
I am.

~ *Unknown*

Chapter Twelve

"Getting over a painful experience is much like crossing monkey bars.
You have to let go at some point in order to move forward."
~ *Unknown*

ACCEPTANCE AND LETTING GO

"Letting go doesn't mean giving up . . . it means moving on. It
is one of the hardest things a person can do . . . We feel that
letting go is giving up, quitting, and that, as we all know, is
cowardly. But as we grow older we are forced to change our
way of thinking. We are forced to realize that letting go means
accepting things that cannot be. It means maturing and moving
on, no matter how hard you have to fight yourself to do so."
~ *Unknown*

My Healing Experience

After the death of Kristo, I went through many stages of personal growth
and healing. I was now at a point at which I was ready to 'let go' and
needed a break from the mundane routines of day-to-day life. I needed
to get away, far away. In February 2004, I returned to Thailand (one
of my favorite countries to visit). Having travelled through Phuket, I

boarded a ferry to one of my favourite islands, Phi-Phi, which is about 40 minutes away by boat. If it is low tide, the long tail boats come out to fetch you and your luggage as you approach the island! Your luggage gets thrown onto the longboat and then you jump in! This is most definitely an experience on its own. Shoes can now be packed away as you alight at the water's edge and make your way up the white beach to the bungalows. It's paradise, and one of the most beautiful sets of islands in the world.

I was at the acceptance and 'letting go' stage of my grief and needed the healing physical touch of another. I found that traditional 'Thai massage', which works the pressure points and re-aligns energy lines in the body, quenched my longing and relieved all the muscle and body aches and pains I had self-inflicted with stress from a build-up of 'lactic acid'.

I would go twice a day just for the sake of the physical touch, whether it was a manicure or pedicure with arm/leg massage or a full body massage. I found touch played a significant part in the healing process. One gets so accustomed to keeping your distance from everyone after death and shutting everyone out that the basic power of touch and hugging is forgotten or not wanted.

I love the peace and tranquility of the remote island surrounded by a coral reef and the stillness of the turquoise waters. I still love the sea and always will, even after this life-changing experience I had been through, but this was a very different sea to me. There were no huge thunderous waves you could hear in the distance, but a quiet, peaceful, tranquil sea. The bigger waves broken by the surrounding coral reef left soft, gentle waves lapping on the white sand of the shore. I would never have been able to do this at the sea where our loss happened. I was basically in a different world, a place I could be at one with myself and with the sea. The perfect scene and right timing for me to accept and 'let go'. I stayed at a hotel with beach bungalows built on the white sand of the island near the water's edge. The walkways to the room where beach sand and water-bowls with deep reddish pink hibiscus flowers lined the way. It was so close to the beauty of nature. Such a beautiful, peaceful and tranquil island with dramatic cliffs that dropped into the ocean in the distance. I was now at peace and at last comfortable with who I was and what I was. The letting go of all my pain and accepting my feelings brought me closer to Kristo.

WHISPER

What if I whispered your name
And in an instant you came?
What if I touched you;
Would it feel the same?

What if you brought me a white rose
And placed the petals around my heart
And then promised me
We would never ever part?

What if you hugged me so tight
And then decided to stay the night?
And in the morning when you leave,
Remind me that this was only a dream . . .

~ Anne Pieterse

Chapter Thirteen

"Compare your griefs with other men's and they will seem less"
~ Spanish Proverb

REVISITING GRIEF

Mother Nature's Destruction

My best healing took place on that island, and I will never forget the welcome and beauty of the people that helped me during my grief. They played a significant part in my healing in the February of 2004. Ten months later, in December 2004, I was devastated and heartbroken to watch the South Asian Tsunami that had just about 'swallowed and destroyed' this beautiful island of Phi-Phi and its people along with many other countries. I had a craving to go back then and there. Unfortunately, I was unable to leave my family and work at this time, but I watched every moment on TV capturing the grief and devastation of the power of the two waves that hit the Phi-Phi Island from different directions. It was awful watching on television from home the tsunami wave come over the pool I had bathed in peacefully a few months before.

Where were the friends I had made, where were their children? I remembered the lady who made me tuna pancakes every lunch time. She lived down the lane from the hotel and used to lay her six children on the floor to sleep. Would they be alive? Would she be alive? I was always greeted with such a welcome and a smile from her. I would wonder over and over again if the children survived and, unfortunately, due to the severity of the destruction, I could most probably expect the very worst. My life felt like it was turned upside down. I was in shock again. Remember that they had helped me through my grief in the first place and now they too were probably gone. I prayed so hard, I felt so much guilt. They had helped me so much with my own grief.

I returned with my family to the island in late December 2005 (a few days before the one year anniversary of the tsunami). It's an island both my husband and I love. This time we took Sarah, our daughter, with. She was six years old at the time.

We arrived at the island in the late afternoon and checked into our bungalow. We then went for a walk to where the Phi Phi Princess Hotel was, where I had enjoyed myself 10 months before and where I had let-go a lot of my pain. There was nothing: the only remaining part of the Hotel was the concrete base in the open hotel reception area on which the 'waterfall fountain feature' stood. That was it! That was all that was left. I couldn't get my bearings, my inner compass felt broken again, a feeling I just find so hard to describe. I couldn't find where my bungalow once stood, nothing. I again felt I had lost all sense of direction. I looked up to the sky, I looked to the remaining palm trees, nothing was where I knew it once had been. I was lost again.

I sat there for an hour trying to orientate myself, but couldn't. It was hopeless: there were no pointers. I gave up. The press had started arriving, came over and talked to me. They asked me if I knew anything about the island and so on, and I told them I had been here 10 months before the tsunami. They asked me if I would do an interview for Japanese TV in the morning at the same spot and I obliged. I would first need to compose myself. The hotel had lost approximately 36 staff members and 100 guests.

Our bungalow was near the local school on the far side of the island. Sitting on the verandah of the bungalow, I couldn't help but see in the early mornings the few remaining school children cycling to school on their own or with a sibling, knowing they had lost their family, their school friends and teachers. The pain was totally incomprehensible. There could only have been a handful of pupils. . . What they saw was horrifying and will never be forgotten. It was too painful staying near the school, and the bungalow only had a fan and was thus very hot. I couldn't take the pain and the heat together; my bravery was diminishing.

The very sight of these young survivors gave me flashbacks and made me more tired, and I always know the benefit of getting a good night's sleep so I can face the next day. I needed somewhere in which I could lock myself away, somewhere cooler, and needed an air-conditioner, so we moved closer to the hub of the island to one of the remaining hotels. We booked into the only remaining hotel and stayed on the third floor to ensure the family's utmost safety. We kept the television on just to keep watch from our room. The Hotel had installed cameras facing both sides of the bay so you could see from your room what was happening outside. God forbid anything happening again, but we had decided should anything happened we could just go higher up into the hotel. There were survival trunks on the top floor. I very much doubted if I would ever go up the new evacuation route on the mountain which was some way behind us. I tried to be brave and switched the television off when retiring to bed at night, praying and hoping for calmness. The remainder of the survivors on the ground had none of this privilege; if they could be brave, then so could I.

My daughter Sarah just loved the Thai massage too, and used sleep for hours afterwards. A few days before the one year commemoration of the tsunami, during the heat of the day, we went down for our usual massage. We were all lying down and having massages in the shop, side by side. After about half an hour, I heard a slight commotion outside the shop and people talking. The next thing all the workers ran and shouted to me 'Mama, tsunami, hurry'. My nickname was 'Mama'. I asked what happened, and they said, 'We thought tsunami', 'We can hear it'.

Picture almost the entire village abandoning their little shops and running up the mountain behind and then coming down about one hour later. I understood where they were coming from. They had started 'reliving the horror' before the first anniversary, visualizing the repetition of events for which they had so much fear. I was good at that, too, and what a frightening time that really is. We were tired by the heat and were enjoying the coolness inside. I could feel the reality of this tsunami, the panic, fear and dread it caused. I reassured them that there were sirens that would go off first, and (supposedly) someone in the watch tower. I tried to pacify them, but they would have none of that.

This tsunami was still very raw to them, very real. The pain and destruction and loss was unimaginable. Not forgetting their own pain from their own injuries and mangled legs as they were still waiting for further surgery. I know the feeling of the build-up to a first anniversary, and every one thereafter. Not like theirs, of course. The first anniversary is the worst, with all the flashbacks and reliving the horror. The other anniversary dates are a little easier as time moves on. You relive the nightmare. It doesn't matter how much you try and disregard it, it plays over and over, gives you panic attacks and leaves you lifeless and consumes all your energy. Grief holds you to ransom. It grips your whole body with fear. I don't know how they ran up the mountain, I guess it was adrenaline.

Nothing can make this fear better. You believe it will happen again, you believe it is happening and that's what I was watching: the fear. I was starting to believe them, that a tsunami was actually coming again, but I had to reassure myself and my family. We had to find our own reality amongst this. We also all agreed when we came to the island that anything could happen and that we would accept each other's deaths if that's what was going to happen. It was our choice to stay there and we chose to remain, fear and all! Reality hit home for me, and I could understand what they were feeling and the replay of the 'motion picture', the replay of the year before and all they had been through. Some had lost all their children, some their children and husbands, some everyone, including their extended families. But most of all they had lost much more than I had: they lost their homes, their possessions, their photos and their loved ones, everything.

I watched their reality building up to the one year anniversary of the tsunami. It was heart-wrenching. We visited the locals we had made friends with day after day. They needed to make a living and we tried supporting them as best we could, and eventually became good friends. Sarah was watched everywhere she went on the island. She was a treasure to them. Everyone knew her and loved her.

Christmas was an excruciatingly painful day for me. Apart from not having my own son with me and experiencing my own and my family's grief on that day, it was very difficult, and we all moved a lot slower. This was the worst Christmas I have ever had. I too was starting to get sucked into the pain. There could be no happiness. We were surrounded by sorrow. The air was warm and smelt like death, the humidity oppressive, and the sun beat down fiercely.

The local and international press had engulfed the island and, along with various organizations such as the Red Cross, was waiting for those who were meeting for the one year anniversary of the tsunami. I was saddened by the lack of help forthcoming from the outside communities for the locals. It was Christmas Day, the day before the one year commemoration on Boxing Day. I was mortified by the frequency of the pain the locals experienced as the scene from the year before seemed to 'replay'. I watched; I listened to them cry. There was nothing to say. All I could do was listen and feel and be with them. I was caught up in a nightmare; I had never seen so much agony and pain in my life.

I thought my own grief was bad, but it did not touch on what I was witnessing. I had only lost one child to the sea, whereas their losses were

WHAT IF I WHISPERED YOUR NAME?

much greater. If they could survive, I thought, well, then so could I. That's when I made the final decision that I would now just going to get on with my life and leave the pain of the past behind. My experience was virtually insignificant compared to theirs. It was a true wakeup call for me, and witnessing what I did reinforced this. It will haunt me for the rest of my life.

The evening eventually came, with the sunset. The island was peaceful, but there was a lingering pain in the air you could hear. I went to see if the locals I had made friends with were okay—just okay was what I was looking for. They weren't. They didn't know how they were going to survive the night: the panic attacks, the fear, the unknown, and then the next day itself. I suggested they get something from the chemist to help them calm down just so they could face the next day. I went to the chemist with a few to ask if they had anything to help them sleep. Before they retired for the night they each took one very light sleeping pill. I made sure they were all comfortable and went back to the hotel, promising them I would be with them as early as I could in the morning to take them to the commemoration.

I woke up exhausted. The heat was unbearable (even though our room was air-conditioned), and the only clothes I could bear to put on were my swimming costume and sarong. There were many foreigners on the island for the commemoration, but what stood out for me was that very few people, if any, were assisting the locals. One young American girl, who was working hard out in the sun assisting with the wall of remembrance, came to mind. Her skin was red and blistered from the sun—there is no time for sun cream and umbrellas when you are helping people in that pain. Believe me, it's the last thing on your mind. My skin was also scorched and blistered, and took a month or so to heal. I had given our umbrellas to those in so much pain. It didn't matter at all though, as this was a very small sacrifice to make for them.

In the morning, we went to fetch the local friends we had made. We walked slowly hand in hand. They did not utter a word. They did not know if they could face the day, but with a little help they succeeded. It was so painful. This was the greatest exhibition of human misery I have ever been a part of. The pain was excruciating. I was pleased that we were leaving the island for another the next morning. I couldn't take one moment more of this pain. Many people stayed on the mainland and just came over to the island for the day. They were wise.

During the week I had asked the ladies if they had touched the sea again and tried to make friends with it. They replied that they had not. Never. I challenged them after the ceremony to go with them to the water's edge. This island is tiny, and the water surrounds it and is nearly always in sight. The ceremony was on the beach, too. There was no getting away from it, whichever way you turned.

The Prime Minister of Krabi arrived in a helicopter with his entourage for the service. After the service he walked around and talked to the children. He presented Sarah with a book called *The Children of Phi Phi Island* which really acknowledged her presence. These are true-life stories of the surviving children on Phi Phi. He inscribed in it for her, and she was very proud that she had been part of this day, sharing their losses and feeling the pain of her own.

Afterwards I tried to persuade just one of them, a lovely young lady who had lost her newly-wed husband to the sea, if she would like to go down and put her feet in the water and throw her flowers into the sea. She was reluctant, but somehow we managed to walk hand in hand. Throwing some flowers she had brought to the ceremony was a catharsis, a way to acknowledge him and the others she had lost to the sea. Then, after about five minutes, turning her back on the pain, we walked up the beach and joined the others who were watching. A catharsis is an emotional release, a purging of emotions, purification and sometimes a release or renewal. Later on in the evening, most of the visitors and locals gathered on the beach to light a lantern. The sky was alight with 1000 lanterns.

Goodnight

Waiting for the sun to set
In the stillness of the bay
Lighting candles
To place in lanterns
Emotions released from the day.

As the lanterns gain height
They bring the sky alight
Reaching higher and higher
Remembering those once loved
Who are not with us tonight.

~ Anne Pieterse

We ended up just about abandoning our holiday to help the locals. Apart from the psychological support (of which they received very little), some of them had lost their livelihood. Rice was the staple dish for the locals at this time. I asked what may have appeared to be a very silly question at the time, but my curiosity got the better of me! I asked what protein they had with the rice. They said either vegetables or chicken, which was more expensive. I then asked them why they didn't eat fish, as it was cheaper and in abundance on and around the island. The answer was very surprising, and one that had never occurred to me. They told me that fish are scavengers, and would have pecked on the bodies that got washed out to sea. This was only one year after the disaster, and I could see the logic in their thinking. I tried to comprehend. I got flashbacks myself, as you can well imagine. I always tried to dismiss the thought of this happening to my son's body. Until now, Sarah has never eaten seafood, and I don't think she ever will. We eat fish very rarely, as she can't stand the smell, but it may perhaps also have something to do with the unconscious thought in her mind about fish. She lost her brother to the sea, and now certainly doesn't want to eat anything from it. I never knew this would have impacted on her from such an early age.

Another Thai couple we met on the island offered us a long-tail boat hire. The skipper's name was 'Red'. After the tsunami, he found his boat miles away, minus the engine. An American couple very kindly purchased an engine for him and he was now able to support his wife and family by taking guests on boat rides to the different islands and fishing expeditions. We hired him for the entire week. His wife used to run a shop, but now she worked in the open under the elements. The same couple bought her a smoothie machine from the mainland and we helped her set up her stall. She was able to source all the local fruit and fresh coconut.

We went to the mainland to purchase stools and tables etc. for her customers to sit on. Empowering people during times of despair and loss of hope is so rewarding. They appreciate everything you do for them. She was afraid to travel to the mainland and go over the water. They were trying to help themselves, but needed the final push. The next day, her business was thriving in the heat. She had also sourced ice for her fruit shakes and had a queue for the fresh fruit smoothies. Things were going so well for her that, before we left, she had developed an ambition to get a new shop once they had finished the small buildings. She would be able to secure a small deposit with the earnings she was making and reserve a shop.

We loved helping the locals and putting our holiday on hold. It's just something you do when you are faced with these incredibly challenging circumstances. I believe nothing crosses your path without a reason. There was a reason for everything.

Sarah fell in love with the island and its people and asked, 'Mommy why can't you just buy this island? I just love it!' She has written a poem for her brother which she would like to share with you too. The brother she misses so very much.

My Angel

You are my missing puzzle piece
Nothing feels right with you not here
Not here by my side
Not here in my sight
Not here in my life.

You were once the one always
Caring for me, playing with me
You always had a cheeky laugh that brought tears of joy
You always had a smile beaming from ear to ear.

You will always be
A very special brother to me
I'm waiting for you patiently,
And I'll always remember that
Sweet last gentle kiss you gave me
Without whispering goodbye.

You always called me your baby Angel,
I have to accept you are theirs now
But I know that you are still watching me from above
Watching over me, like a lily-white dove.

Take me soaring to the heavens above
Hold me under your wings of love
Let's play and dance through the skies
And tip-toe round the clouds
As we remember our very special love.

I know you will always be a part of me
And I am thinking of you endlessly
Of the day we can be together
And share our dreams forever.
I love you so much!

~ Sarah Pieterse

What I have learnt

- I learnt some very good and lifelong lessons on that island.
- I have only experienced one death of a child at one time, so when I look around and see the pain of others, I do not feel alone.
- I now reflect on those who have lost their homes and entire families and belongings.
- For me one of the biggest lessons of the South Asian Tsunami was that, 'If others could survive such great losses, surely I could survive the loss of one child?' What was wrong with me? I have seen them and felt their immeasurable pain, so when I am feeling low I reflect on this. It helps me put my own grief and life into perspective very fast. Their losses are unfathomable.
- I have sat in a support group with two people who experienced multiple losses of children that were too tragic to mention, and I can only respect them and wonder where and how they found the strength to carry on. You are all very, very brave and I admire you and count my blessings. I feel so deeply for you. I know that the courage you find to talk about your loss helps others reflect on their own loss. I acknowledge your excruciating pain and admire your strength and courage to carry on. My heart bleeds for you. Rich blessings and love to you.
- Sharing and listening intimately to other's pain and stories makes one connect and self-reflect.
- Death is death, no matter what the cause, grief is grief. No one's grief is any worse than another's, excluding the multiple deaths, of course. I haven't experienced them personally, so I can't write about them.
- Death is final—end of story—**final**. It's the only thing we can be certain of.

Chapter Fourteen

TRANSFORMATION THROUGH CREATIVITY

"A journey of a thousand miles begins with a single step"
~ Unknown

Creativity

I found that creativity played an important part in my healing. Try and unlock your own creative energy. This could be one by joining a yoga class, exercise class, taking interest in your garden again, going for walks or perhaps keeping a dream/feelings journal. We need to get our creativity back. Do the hobbies you once enjoyed, start showing an interest in them again. You may enjoy painting or drawing, creative writing, poetry or even pottery.

Journal

What is very helpful to express feelings you don't want to share with others is writing and keeping your own journal. In the mornings I used to wake up and write what was on my mind or what feelings I was feeling deep down inside, I would write, scribble, get my anger down on paper and later on in the day go and burn it. I felt enormous relief. For those that can keep a journal without your family peeking into it are lucky! I was not this fortunate and preferred to burn mine and felt a release after doing this too.

Self-Esteem

There is a great loss of self after death. We actually lose a part of ourselves, our self-esteem and our identity. We feel hopeless, depressed and guilty. I felt like a victim for a very long time.

I was in victim mode, loved depression and couldn't get out of this 'role'. I had an addiction, *I was addicted to depression.* I never told my grief counselor this, but she was no fool either: I was just too ashamed to admit this but have found the courage now to share this.

Positive Affirmations

When your self-esteem is low and you think everyone is on your case, I found that using positive affirmations was a useful tool. We manifest what we think. If we think negatively we become negative, if we think positively we too can become positive.

Affirmations work like magic. They ground and centre you straight away. Affirmations and prayers are both ways of asking for divine guidance.

I have my own very special affirmation, and you too can find yours or make one up to suit you.

Use it however often you need to, every minute, every hour, every day, and you will see the positive change. **Here are just a few examples:**

~ I am good enough
~ I am special
~ I now let pain out, and let God in
~ I give you my pain, but keep my love for (name)
~ I choose to heal, I choose love
~ I love and accept myself in every way unconditionally
~ My life is moving in a positive direction
~ I am master of my own destiny
~ I shine as bright as the full moon on a cloudless night
~ I am brave, have courage and will fight on

Identifying your Archetype

Just as fairytales portray different characters such as the victim, villain and hero, so do we in our own lives. When we have got rid of all our unnecessary 'clutter' and spring-cleaned our mind and made space, this allows us to explore and increase our level of consciousness creatively just like a fairytale. We can be aware of which character we are playing or which character we may be 'stuck' in. Archetypes are something we all experience and know intimately from the inside. Archetypes are responsible for the persistent themes we see surfacing in our own lives. I didn't know the different archetypes until I studied them. I didn't know any different, didn't know that you can chose to be the magician, healer, jester or the hero, or choose to change which role you are acting out. There are many different archetypes and it interesting to see how they can influence you to change your patterning.

'*All the world's a stage, and all the men and women merely players*'
~ *William Shakespeare*

Learning the different archetypes allowed me to explore and try working with and feeling the benefits of changing my behaviour. This was very interesting, but I didn't want to make a change. I was only used to the 'Victim' mode, that's all I really knew and acted out, but I was challenged by myself to try another character, the Magician. I had spent much of my life in 'Caregiver' and 'Victim' mode. 'Magician' worked well for a while, but then something awoke 'the Hero' inside of me and I learnt how to become a 'Hero'. Now I have moved on to become 'a Warrior' and 'Hero of the Warrior'. Those are my own words by the way! But to have mastered grief in my own way and through my own experiences and hope to be able to inspire others to overcome the fears that grief brings and join in the fight.

Guided Imagery

This has a wonderfully relaxing effect during your grief, and you really feel refreshed and cleansed afterwards. It can also aid in letting-go and letting-be. Guided imagery involves listening to calm, soothing music and being guided into imagery by the speaker, where the mind can relax and allow fresh ideas and feelings to surface. I will be going into more of this in my second book so am just skimming the surface for now.

There are many self-help books, CDs and downloads available, or you could be creative and write your own or listen to your own serene music.

Music

Music is creativity for our brain, a bit like 'brain gym'. It wakes, soothes, calms and refreshes our soul. It speaks volumes. You too can create your own music, even if it's out of tune. Have you ever seen an angry person whistling? I used to have a boyfriend who would whistle every morning when he got up to make the tea! It was chirpy as could be energizing and positive. Try something, anything, to make your own music. It could be drumming, singing, or just listening. Our entire energetic system is influenced by sounds and responds to tones and frequencies. Music shifts energies immediately and is relaxing.

Feeling Nature's Energy

Fling the curtains open in summer and let the golden rays of the sun flood into the room or follow a few raindrops falling down the window. Watch the raindrops form ripples as they drop into a pond. Whatever you do, 'be present and feel present'. This is necessary and important if you want to feel energy in a positive way. Now is the only time we have, use of it: be conscious, have an even deeper awareness.

Chapter Fifteen

EPILOGUE:

STARING DEATH IN THE FACE

"Hope is Grief's Best Friend"

~ Anne Pieterse

Just like a 'fairytale', some of which have a 'tragic ending' and some of which have a 'lived happily ever after' ending, I am happy to say that my story has got a happy ending! For the time being, at least; life is fragile and can change at any moment.

Jason was born with an incurable genetic disease, Cystic Fibrosis, which affects mainly the respiratory and digestive system. From the age of three months, being very ill much of the time and constantly admitted to Hospital and ITU with recurrent chest infections, he has defied all the odds to survive.

We were told that Jason would not live to the age of six. One day in ITU a mother of another child asked me why I didn't consider putting my son in a home or giving him up for adoption. She went on to say that I would never be able to live life with a child whose care regime took most of my time plus the constant Hospitalisation and Intravenous Therapy. Why in the world would I ever consider doing that, I thought? I was going to live with the hand I was dealt, come hell or high water! The insensitive and thoughtless things people do say!

74

When Jason had reached the age of about fifteen, a new 'breakthrough' drug was released which we decided to use. We had to pay for this medication, but we made the decision to keep him on one of the most expensive drugs (in those days about 550 pounds a month) to help ease his breathing and the severity of chest infections. This drug was Dornase Alfa, which is a genetically engineered form of the human enzyme DNAse. This protein breaks down excess DNA in the pulmonary secretions of people with cystic fibrosis. We were going to take any treatment we could possibly afford to keep him alive to give him the best quality of life and ensure that he had an excellent chance for a transplant. Our attempts were not in vain as he managed to reach a 'CF' healthy twenty-four years. (What I mean by 'healthy' here is to be mentally and physically fit enough for a double lung transplant. Only certain CF adults/children are able to have a transplant, as there is a very strict protocol and points system to qualify for transplant.)

By the age of twenty-three Jason had reached the 'terminal stage' of Cystic Fibrosis. He was facing death, as were we. Knowing what it felt like to lose a child, I certainly did not want to lose another. It would have been the death of me. I have watched other women who have lost two children and didn't think I could survive the pain at all.

I was never 'privileged' to have any respite or help with his care, never had carers or nurses, but just went along solo, doing all I could, in the best possible way I could. My only respite from nursing him, from infancy to adulthood, was when he was admitted to Hospital for treatment. His admissions were a stay minimum of two weeks, and got more frequent when he became multi-resistant to the antibiotics that were suppressing his lung infections. I worked during the day and came home at night exhausted, still having to mix dangerous antibiotic cocktails, which were fed in intravenously into his body, to keep him alive. For many years I had been kept awake with his coughing fits and asthma attacks during the night, making it very difficult to get a good nights sleep.

His condition deteriorated even more and he became thinner and thinner, the disease ruthless and zapping up all his weight and energy, leaving him frail and weak and very susceptible to further infections and exposed to death.

At twenty-four we were told that he was now at the end stage of the disease. Being hospitalised for weeks at a time, his condition rapidly deteriorated with life-threatening infections. Jason was being kept alive on intravenous drugs pumped into his body at home day and night and was supported by oxygen. His continuous chronic lung infections, coughing fits, asthma attacks and hyper-reactive airways disease made it virtually impossible for him to leave the house, The simple everyday necessities of sleeping, talking, cooking, eating and walking, are just some of things a healthy person would take for granted that he found it almost impossible to do.

He started becoming dehydrated as he became too weak to eat, and the specialists decided the only way to keep him alive would be to insert a 'Peg Tube' into his stomach. This would boost his food intake and calories. The feeds would be 'nocturnal', run for eight hours during the night to help nourish his body. One of the criteria for acceptance for a double lung transplant was to have a weight of over 50kg. He was balancing on 46-47 kg, which is about 7.4 stone or 103 pounds. We first had to build his weight and strength up before they would even consider him for a transplant.

We succeeded and his weight gradually built up over a few months. However, every life-threatening lung infection would set him back again and his body would lose weight. Now, when his body was ready on most levels to have the first interview for transplant, we had an appointment during which we would be told what transplant was all about, the pros and cons and so on, and whether the Doctors thought Jason would survive.

Transplant is all about how fit you are for surgery, whether or not you are a suitable candidate, whether or not your body would survive the trauma of the operation, and if the transplant would be successful. They look at the possibility of success and the future quality of life, and if they think you are not going to make it, will not even go further with any discussions. Your FeV1 (lung function) has to be between certain parameters to even be considered for transplant.

With Jason's oxygen levels and body weight declining fast, and him being unable to walk upstairs, or any distance, his body weight and health was balancing on the borderline for acceptance for final transplantation. Hence, every moment of his rigorous therapy and peg tube feeding continuously at night played an important part in helping him keep alive.

I remember this appointment being in about January. The risks of surgery were explained. Between the two of us, we could see nothing positive about the two hour talk; we found everything negative. We knew this was 'the end', there were no guarantees that lung transplantation would work and we knew that only a small handful of CF patient's survived such an operation. At that stage, we only knew how many patient's had died on the theatre table, or within a week, or a few months after. We didn't know anything about the positives.

The choice was up to Jason. The parent/carer was not allowed to influence the decision at all. I basically had nothing to do with the decision. Jason was an adult now, they left the choice up to him and he was terrified at this idea. He eventually decided to change his mind. This was too frightening, and he would not be going down the transplant route. I prayed and prayed desperately and clung on to any hope I had left. I could not force him. I myself did not know which would be the better option. One of the major contributing factors was that he was very weak and not well, and couldn't think clearly. His coughing was continuous; he was tired, he was so busy using his remaining energy to keep alive and to keep breathing that it's very difficult to think straight. Not forgetting that he was facing his own death too.

After six months, he changed his mind, he became more positive about the idea of the transplant as he knew he was dying and had nothing to lose. He had been talking over the internet to other transplant survivors and went on to meet some. He had also heard that you can always turn the call down or go off the list. This is not what he had wanted to do, but he wanted to know that he could opt out in case he had too much fear and changed his mind at the last minute. The list was long, and there were about a hundred patients waiting for transplant already. We would wait another two months for an appointment at the Harefield Transplant Hospital, and so, all in all, this extension after his initial refusal made the total wait another eight months.

In early August 2009 I took him up to the Transplant Hospital for assessment and to meet the team. This was a two-hour trip each way. Portable oxygen in car, off we went and both felt so positive. This was an amazing day, a day of so much hope and inspiration. He was now on a lung function of 10%. Again he was told of the severity of the operation and also that the donor organ would have to be a perfect match. The Transplant Team would start taking more blood from him for tissue typing etc. and to see what blood group he was. Lucky for Jason he is A positive, the best blood category to be in, as the most organ donations are received from this group. Luck was on our side at last. He had a better chance of transplant now.

After the hour-long consultation, the Transplant Surgeon got up and shook Jason's hand and mine and welcomed us with open arms into the Harefield family (as they call it). I felt relieved: they had obviously accepted Jason. We were both so overjoyed at how positive they were and felt help was at hand.

Jason received a phone call the next week to say he was on the Transplant List. We didn't think too much of it because it was only a 'possibility' and didn't really ever think this would turn out to be real. I think as a mother I was in denial but also grounded, as Jason was dying and anything could stop the transplant process. He was facing his own mortality and I was contemplating the possibility of losing another son. He could get a severe infection at any time or perhaps pick up Swine Flu, to which he was more susceptible to now in his weakened state during the winter. He could lose more weight, which, in turn, would mean that he would be taken off the list, or even not get the opportunity to receive donated organs or even die. This was the reality of it. It was 'bittersweet'. I hated thinking into the future and planning ahead, as I had already learnt that future dreams for your children could be shattered at any moment. I was trying to live from moment to moment and enjoy as best I could his last days and care for him in the best possible way I could.

I tried to remain positive throughout this time, as grieving is a continual process you go through when you are losing someone so dear to you. You are on edge for every phone call that you hear. I continued to work and try to live as normally as possible. About 3 months later, I was at work one day at four pm, just about ready to pack up for the day. I work about 45 minutes from home. Jason was at home with my mum. He phoned me to say he had a call from the Transplant co-coordinators and he had accepted the call. He could hardly speak, he was in shock. I told him to go without me. My mum went with him in the ambulance, and they were 'blue lighted' to Harefield.

No time can be wasted when you receive a possible call. You have to drop everything you are doing, organise an ambulance and go. The whole process from the call to the Hospital and then waiting to see if the donated organs match and are suitable can take anything from four to eight hours. Every occasion you accept a call (and on your arrival at the Hospital) you need to be fully prepared for theatre, have a total wash down with disinfectant in the shower, get dressed for theatre, and then the long wait begins. This was a trial run, so to speak. However, the donor organs were not suitable and we all returned home.

We received at least eleven possible transplant calls over a two-month period. December and January was hectic. On one of the calls, the ambulance refused to take him as he was just too weak and they didn't have enough oxygen on board. With two of the calls we were turned back before we had even reached the Hospital. The other nine calls the 'whole procedure' of showering and decontaminating before theatre was done every time.

This took a lot of energy and a toll on Jason's health. The stress was unbelievable. He was readmitted to Hospital. If he was admitted to treat an infection he would not be a priority on the transplant list, and would not receive a call whilst on treatment. His treatments in Hospital took a minimum of 14 days.

This was to be our last Christmas together in 2009. We prepared for the worst. From what I had been told by the Specialists, I knew his time was running out fast. Jason had received a call two days before Christmas and two days after. This gave me little time to prepare the meal for Christmas. He was hardly able to eat and relied on being tube fed. We were exhausted, as each possible transplant call and response to took us at least twelve hours, which included our travelling there and back. Celebrating Christmas was not important, saving Jason's life was. He had to be transported by Ambulance as he was too weak to travel with us in the car. He felt safer, more secure and in control as it is very difficult receiving these calls. He also needed 'blue lighting', whereas we could not speed or go through traffic lights. The timeframe you are given from the minute you receive and accept the possible transplant organs and the time to get to the Hospital were for us sometimes one hour sometimes one and a half hours. Living two hours away this was complicated to say the least. I cannot imagine what thoughts were going through his head: was this day the day he was going to live or die, would this be his last day. It was a chance you take, it was the only chance for survival.

I used to sit in the front of the Ambulance with the driver trying to co-ordinate the safe arrival of Jason within the time frame given by the Hospital. It was winter, the roads dangerous, black ice, frost, snow, the Ambulance trying to plough through the snow, some of the roads closed off and some lanes on the highway blocked due to road works.

Chapter Sixteen

MIRACLES

*"Don't think of organ donation as giving up part of you to keep a
total stranger alive.
It's really a total stranger giving up almost all of themselves to keep
part of you alive".*

~ *Unknown*

One night after returning from Harefield, going to work that day and
coming home early exhausted to rest. I was just putting Jason to bed. As
the family sat in the lounge that evening my mother said to me that if he
didn't get a call tonight she would doubt if he would be alive tomorrow.
That's how dire the situation was. I agreed with her but had to focus
on keeping him comfortable and nourished so that he wouldn't be too
weak for the transplant. We had to wait up later as the pump for his
tube feed's alarm kept going off so we wouldn't be able to sleep with the
noise and he had to have a nocturnal feed to remain alive. We waited up
till 11pm for a replacement pump and I had just hooked him up with
the feeding set and bottle through the new pump, when less than ten
minutes later, when I got into bed, the phone rang. Exhausted to the
bone, I ran downstairs to answer the phone. Of course I knew who it
was: only the Hospital used the home phone. This would be his eleventh
transplant call, which came at 11pm on a snowy winter's night in January
2010.

80

At this stage we were on first name basis with the transplant co-ordinators and knew each other well. I answered; they asked to speak to Jason. He couldn't speak, he was exhausted, needed sleep and had switched off his mobile phone, he had had enough. They told me that there was another possibility of donor organs. I asked them to wait while I went up to speak to him. He was the one who had to decide on the call. He said **no**, I argued with him and told him that nothing was going to stop us now. We couldn't give up now, we had come so far and hope was a breath away. It may just be the call that would save his life. After much convincing him just to stay where he was and that I would organise and get him down the steps, and he could try and rest/sleep in the ambulance, he finally gave in. I said 'yes' on the phone and then had to call 999 to arrange an ambulance, then go and try and dress him as he was just too weak and it was so cold and snowing outside.

Jason frail and weak, desperately needing his tube feed as we had started late and had to stop all feed and drinks prior to surgery. This left him weakened.

The ambulance staff arrived, I showed them for the first time to his bed upstairs, as he was too weak to walk down the steps, and they helped him down. We had a blanket around him, they placed him gently on the stretcher and into the ambulance. Off we went again to Harefield. This was the final call.

I prepared him for theatre: again the shower, disinfectant, etcetera, in the bathroom through the icy winter, and made him comfortable while we waited for the 'go ahead'.

I was at the Hospital, Andre with me, too exhausted to move, but the adrenaline kicked in and takes over. I said my last goodbye to Jason as he was wheeled into Theatre at three am in the morning. We still weren't sure if the transplant would go ahead, as this was the 'unknown' part of transplant. The patient can get anaesthetised and opened up before surgery whilst they await the donor organs. The old organs are not removed yet at this stage, because there is a limited amount of time before the donor organs can be re-transplanted. The organs have to be transplanted, as I believe, within four hours of them being harvested.

So Jason could have woken up after being anaesthetised should the transplant not have gone ahead. We all knew this and prepared ourselves for any eventuality.

We went back to his private ward just in case the transplant did not go ahead. Until the donor organs have arrived at the Hospital and been re-checked, there is still no confirmation until the Surgeon's are totally happy to carry on with the Surgery. The operation could be called off at any time. I just prayed and prayed, and again tried to just 'let be and let

God'. I couldn't take anymore. I was healthy, and I felt exhausted. Jason must have felt terrible after sleepless nights and all the stress the calls had created. We were eventually told at 4.30am that everything was ok and Jason had the 'green light' for transplant to go ahead.

Andre and I managed to get into the Hospital's Accommodation where I would go and rest a while and try and get some much needed sleep. But with all the adrenaline going there is little time for that. I didn't have a bag or a change of clothes with me. The most important thing at that stage was just to save Jason's life, nothing else mattered.

At eleven am I was dozing and received a call from ITU. The transplant was finished and I could go through and see Jason. I was so relieved I couldn't get to him fast enough. I just couldn't believe he had survived the surgery and was fearful of what I would see, and yet so elated that it was over at last and that he had a good chance of surviving.

Jason received his first double lung transplant and was in theatre for 8 hours. His transplant was 'uneventful' and he was awake by midday. All appeared well and Jason was breathing with the aid of oxygen and had started eating in the late evening and was talking. The Surgeons were equally amazed that he had survived and all of us were very proud too. He was very pale and I was a little concerned. I didn't know what to expect, but he looked more comfortable than I had imagined.

Three hours after the transplant the ventilator was removed and Jason was breathing on his own. When we arrived back after lunch, we found him sitting upright in the chair next to his bed. He was texting on his mobile phone and would communicate with us by writing as his throat was sore from the ventilator and all the pipes that had been down there during surgery.

On the second day the physiotherapists came and brought in a foot-pedalling machine. Jason had the strength to do about ten minutes intermittently on this without becoming breathless. I was amazed at his strength.

Later the same afternoon Jason's condition started deteriorating and he was put on oxygen to improve his saturation levels. They were declining fast and he was put back on the Ventilator for his new lungs to rest. Three days later, after experiencing a severe infection, Jason's condition became critical.

The Harefield Transplant Team decided the best option would be to place Jason on ECMO (Extracorporeal membrane oxygenation), which is similar to a heart—lung machine, to keep him alive. ECMO was a major procedure and they would have to take Jason back to theatre. They needed to divert the blood out of Jason's body through a thick pipe in his groin and into a machine which would filter and oxygenate the

WHAT IF I WHISPERED YOUR NAME?

blood and then return it to his body through what looked like a hosepipe in his neck. Again, this was major surgery, and I was not prepared for this. I didn't know what someone on ECMO would even look like. This was unrehearsed for me and caught me unaware. I agreed to the surgery and he was out of theatre at about eleven am that day, as he was listed as an emergency and would be first on their list.

To be honest, the trauma of this time made me forget what happened, so I rely on Andre's input on this. We were waiting in the waiting room outside the access to ITU and had finally received a call that the operation was finished, which meant Jason was still alive. Andre decided that he would go in and see Jason. He told me to wait. (I can't say he is the bravest of all men, as he hates the site of blood and even passed out in the Delivery Room when I was having Kristo)! He came back about five minutes later and told me I was not to go near Jason. He was expecting me to have a coronary if I saw what Jason looked like. He told me that 'it looks like a bus had run over him'. There was fresh blood everywhere, and his hair was full of blood. The surgeons had made a large incision near the base of the right side of his neck and had inserted what looked like a clear 'hosepipe' pumping blood back into his body. There were stitches around the hosepipe, but the blood still leaked everywhere.

After the operation, I was called on my mobile phone. The surgeon who performed the ECMO surgery now wanted to speak to me. I was to meet him in a special waiting room in ITU. Andre and I were together. Things happen so fast when they are trying to save lives; action first, it seems, and then they talk after. I don't even remember signing the papers for ECMO, I don't think there was time. I just told the Surgeons and trusted them to do what needed to be done. There was a Senior Head ITU nurse waiting in the room for him to arrive. I was worried, and thought there was a major problem and Jason was not going to survive and they were going to tell me the worst. I couldn't understand why the nurse was also there. I had drunk two coffees while waiting.

The Surgeon I had initially met on the day of our first appointment when he welcomed us to the Harefield family walked in. I decided to tape the conversation because I know I wasn't going to hear clearly through all my pain and was worried that I would miss something. He rattled on for about ten minutes and then, when he had got my attention, told me in no uncertain terms that *'I was not going to see Jason awake'* again unless there was a miracle. They had to paralyse him with drugs to keep him still and he would be heavily anaesthetised during the duration of ECMO to keep him alive.

He went on to tell us about all the risks of ECMO. I didn't really know what to do at that stage, I was just numb. I had lost control as a mother (again) and I couldn't reverse what had happened. Jason's life was out of my hands and he was being kept alive medically. The risks were:

- *Bleeding, Infection, Blood Transfusions, Clots, Stroke, Renal failure.*

There would be a 'Perfusionist' (A Specialist who operates a heart lung machine) as well as other staff monitoring him on this machine constantly 24/7. They had cleared the entire left wing of ITU for Jason, and reserved all the machinery and staff to deal with him.

Jason was on ECMO for seven long days and nights. During this time he was in an induced coma, fighting for his life. Time was running out fast. He went into acute renal failure on two occasions during ECMO.

After being placed on ECMO, the Surgeons, who had hourly talks with us, informed us that Jason's only hope of survival would be a second lung transplant. They had never done this within 30 days successfully before, but it was our only option.

There would only be a 20% chance of surviving the operation. Now, that's not a great percentage, is it, if you think about it carefully? If he survived the surgery, he would only have a 20% chance of surviving 30 days. If he survived the 30 days he would have a good chance and if he survived another five months without infection he would have a greater chance of living. The chances of survival were very slim. His life expectancy after a second transplant would drop to between 1-5 years.

The choices were to either switch the machines off or wait for the Hospital approval for a second transplant. Pressure was on the Surgeons, as they told us in no uncertain terms that they were not allowed to carry out the operation if they thought Jason did not have a very good chance of survival. They had to have another meeting and talk to their colleagues all over the world. I watched them on their mobile phones. They had sleepless nights over Jason in their battle to keep him alive. We put all our trust and faith into the Transplant Team.

After about three days on ECMO he acquired a Hospital bug. He was later moved to a private room in ITU. His condition started deteriorating slowly and he became less responsive if I talked to him. I still kept playing his favourite music as I think this is so important and helps calm the air and bring a little normality back from all the noise and alarms of ITU.

I drove home and left Andre at the Hospital. I thought I could at least have one night on my own. My back was sore. I needed some normality in my life: just one day away from alarms and machines buzzing and listening to every breath on the ventilator. I wasn't home one hour when Andre called me from the Hospital. He told me to come back immediately; Jason's condition was deteriorating fast. I knew all hope was now lost.

I knew I was facing the death of another son I loved so much. Why? Why was life being so cruel to me? I found no answers. I went through Jason's wardrobe, my heart pounding, the tears spilling everywhere. I had at least a two-hour drive back to the Hospital. I fetched my Mom and Sarah to come with to say goodbye to Jason. That's the stage we were at. I had to think ahead logically and started packing clothes for his funeral. What would they dress him in, what would he have liked, his body so weak, frail and bruised, what could I dress him in? I chose a long-sleeved soft shirt my brother had sent him from the States, comfortable track suit pants and his clean trainers, which hadn't walked anywhere.

We locked up the house and I drove back to the Hospital, Andre calling me all the time to hurry up because I would hit the peak hour traffic on the highway and not get back in time to say goodbye. I can never tell you the state we were all in. I put some music on in the car and put my foot on the accelerator and just drove. It felt as if it took an entire day. The Hospital seemed so far away. I was shaking, every bit of me trembling, as I prepared myself to face another death.

Jason was now placed on the National emergency transplant list. That meant that, should be there have been another donor from the same blood group, he would be the first to receive the organs. Time was now running out fast and we had to prepare for the worst case scenario. My Mom and Sarah had said their last goodbyes to him and went back to the room as it was too much for them to be in ITU for too long a period. Early evening the Surgeons had spoken to us again to tell us that Jason's condition was deteriorating rapidly. I held his hand and kissed his forehead, blood spilling everywhere from ECMO, and I paused. I whispered to him and said 'Jason, are we going to keep fighting.' Although he was in an induced coma, there were times he could respond to us. I waited. It took a few moments and then he nodded his head twice. My confidence felt restored, his courage washed over me. I remembered the 'Award of Courage' he received in his final year at school. He is not a person who gives up and has indestructible strength. That immediately reassured me and instantly gave me another spurt of energy. Adrenaline filled me up and I had reason to keep fighting with him and for him. I made a coffee and drowned my sorrows as the tears refilled my cup. That was a sacred moment for me and I was showered with strength. I had something to cling onto: his wishes.

I was sitting in the private room with him. It was about six pm. I was thinking, praying, holding his hand and wondering. Then, out of the corner of my eye to my left, I watched as one of the two Surgeons peeped their head into the glass window (to see if I was with Jason). They weren't looking at him, they were looking at me. You seem to know if someone is looking for you, I did at that time. I just saw the one Surgeons turquoise eyes light up and then saw him nod at the Head Transplant Surgeon while he rummaged quickly through the steel drawers outside for consent papers. I knew what they were doing: there was a possibility of another donor. You just seem to know. I could see the rush and excitement in their eyes and maybe a slight positive smile. The doors burst open, they informed me that there was a possibility of another donor, and flapped the papers in front of me for consent. So many forms, I can't begin to tell you. I wanted to spend my last moments with him carefully, and now a pile of papers.

I told them I had already signed for another transplant. They informed me that bureaucratic protocols wouldn't allow another double lung transplant; it would have to be bilateral sequential single lung transplants. (The first transplant, for those of you who are interested, was a bilateral sequential double lung transplant.) So I had more paperwork to sign for left and right lung. I couldn't see, the tears of joy washed over me again, I just said 'yes' and signed. Don't know how I managed to hold a pen without shaking and I bet if I looked at those paper's today, they would probably look as though they were left out in the rain! Ink smudged, paper washed with tears of hope, what a mess.

I would far have preferred (well, I didn't have a choice) for him to die on the Theatre table than in front of me with the machines being switched off. That was exactly where I was in my thinking. I could not watch another child die in front of me. I would go mad

The Surgeons had gone out as they promised and returned a few hours later with an update. The lungs were a good match and the other team were harvesting and they would start preparing for Theatre. It was about ten pm now. I was exhausted, finished. I looked at the ITU nurse looking after Jason and told her I was going to bed. I said my final goodbyes; I needed time for my body, too.

We went back to our room, which is about 200 metres from the main Hospital. They asked if they should phone me again at two am before he was due for theatre so I could come and see him again. I told them they could just go ahead. They didn't need me in the way of all this machinery, I was sure, nor did they need to see all my emotions. They had their emotions too to deal with. Transplant is a very emotional time for everyone involved, including the Surgeons and the Harvesting Team. Don't think they don't have emotions; they have many. I have been with them and watched them and listened to their stories. They are also human and show it too.

The lungs were a good match and the surgeons worked tirelessly throughout the night. They promised me that they were non-smoker's lungs and the Head Surgeon assured me he would go with the harvesting team to double check that the donor organs would be a suitable for Jason.

The size of the organs are very important. Jason has quite a small frame and is short, and they hence needed to check the lungs were not too large for the size of his chest.

Father Stanley popped in on his evening round. He had heard what was going on and walked in with his usual smile, which could light up the whole room. He took out what looked like a small gold pot to give Jason the holy sacrament with holy oil. He was administering the last rites in preparation for passing over to eternal life. When he had finished the prayers with the oils anointing Jason's body, he turned to me and said 'This is the eve of Our Lady of Lourdes day'. *Mmmm,* I thought to myself, *well that's a good omen!* A little spark of faith at the moment I needed it! I had always wanted to take Jason to Lourdes for healing. I had prayed so hard for a miracle, everyone had. Could this be the closest to Lourdes I would ever get? Was this going to be the one holy anointing of a sick person I was going to witness with my own eyes? A miracle? I had always believed in miracles, but Jason was on his way out and I don't know what I was thinking at the time. The Minister told us he would see us in Church at nine am the next morning.

I went to bed, I slept, and received a phone call at two am asking if I would like to come up before Jason went to theatre. I declined. It was snowing heavily, I had to keep healthy too and look after myself as best I could. I was sick with the flu at this stage and incredible mentally tired as I had been tested to the limit. I trusted the team and the transplant co-ordinator as they had become as close as family and asked her to go with him to Theatre until he was fully under anaesthetic. She promised me she would be there with the rest of the wonderful team.

What a mess our room in the Hospital accommodation was. Sarah was lying on the floor on a folded duvet, we were cramped in a tiny room—they only have two single beds—but we were all together, a symbol of our strength and unity. We lived like this for weeks and then months. Sarah's sleep was continually interrupted as she kept getting woken up by the calls I was receiving from the Hospital as they went through the different stages of the donor organs and kept updating me.

The following morning we all went to Church to hear the wonderful service on miracles. We stayed a while and prayed whilst we waited for the outcome of the Transplant. I was shivering: the Church was not heated, it was snowing, and I was frozen to the bone. I was mentally numb but there certainly was hope and faith all around us and in the air. I felt like I was walking on clouds, as if I was being carried.

My mobile rang. It was the Hospital. Jason was out of Theatre and back in ITU. He had miraculously survived his second transplant in fewer than twenty days. We drove back to the Hospital and waited to get into ITU. Jason looked like a rag doll lying on the bed, his chest exposed, open and closed again under the same clam shell incision that he first had. (They now cut right across the bottom of your rib cage, in a clam-like style, from left to right, and open the chest up like a bonnet). His appearance was startling: the holes from all the drains and pipes, ECMO now off, no machines making noises, only the ventilator breathing for him.

What a relief, but I still wasn't convinced he would make it. I was elated, but not convinced he would still survive. I kept praying day and night. A re-transplant in a cystic fibrosis patient in under 20 days has apparently never been successful and we are lead to believe that Jason is a world first.

Two months later spring had arrived, and the first daffodils had started opening. Jason was moved out of ITU into HDU. Jason was still not in the clear, but after fighting infection and respiratory failure yet again, he was now on the road to full recovery. His tracheotomy was removed on the morning of his twenty-fifth birthday last year. He had taken his first breath and he could now breathe unassisted. It took him a while to adjust, but he could not believe it. At first he thought he was not breathing and started to panic, but through lots of reassurance he realised there was little effort now to breathe, it just came naturally. Jason was finally allowed out of Hospital for the afternoon to celebrate his birthday on the 17th of April.

At the end of April 2010, Jason was finally discharged after spending three months in Harefield. One year later today we are celebrating his 26th Birthday. He has chosen to stay at home so we can relax and BBQ in the sun and then go down to the beach in the afternoon for a walk. Enjoying the simple pleasures of being alive.

I have now found it possible to write this story, having processed all the emotions of the transplant. It is very difficult. Jason lives on and is very healthy now, eats us out of house and home, and still doesn't know how he survived. He has not been hospitalised once since being discharged, which is nearly a full year.

Although he has had quite a few difficulties adjusting to the levels from his anti-rejection drugs and side effects, this is a small price to pay for survival, being able to breathe unassisted and to have no more life-threatening lung infections.

He is now able to live and experience life without constantly being reminded of illness. He is no longer ill, he is normal and it is taking all of our brains quite a while to adjust to a new life with him ALIVE.

This story and happy ending would not have been made possible without the generous gift from the organ donors and their families. We thank them from the bottom of our hearts for their donations and will be eternally grateful. To all those parents reading this book who have perhaps donated organs of their loved ones, I admire your strength and generosity and I thank you personally.

Chapter Seventeen

"Though no one can go back and make a brand new start, anyone
can start from now and make a brand new ending"

~ Unknown

SURVIVAL

Many people have asked me 'How did you do it?' or have said 'I don't
know how you survived what you have been through'.

These are only people who know a fraction of the second half of my
life, and nothing about this first part.

Well, all I can honestly say is that it took a lot of hard work. I have
been and I have seen with my own eyes. This has been the single most
important assignment of my life, a bit like studying for a 'Master's degree'.
Many hours of reading, research, studying, listening to the great masters
and teachers of the world and finding my own path, sticking to it and
trusting the process. I have mastered grief now in my own way and have
finally written my 'book' or thesis of 30,000 words! I chose to embrace
the path of grief and am so blessed to see the light at the end of the
tunnel, somewhat like 'paving the yellow brick road with bricks of gold'
and then finding the rainbow.

There have been many deviations, many diversions, many dead-ends,
many rocks to trip over, may falls. I fell down and fell again trying to get
up, and many mountains in front of me. I got lost on many occasions,
lost hope too many times to mention, but something sustained me from

within. I found inner strength, courage and determination and together I embraced them and they became my friends.

Many people have worse stories to tell, and far worse life experiences. One only has to be close enough and engaged to listen and feel their pain, or near enough to hear, to realize that yours may not seem so bad after all.

More often than not, I find myself 'lost for words' when I am asked *'How did you do it?'* This question is always unexpected, and, also, why would anyone be interested enough to ask me this question? So I decided to write this book to answer that question, as verbally it would take me far too long, and they would give up listening! I do get mental blocks if I reflect back. I am human, and multiple traumas have affected me.

However, to answer this question on 'How I did you do it'? I would much rather share this beautiful poem by David Whyte, which says it all in nine beautifully written lines. Every time I am asked this question I honestly smile, and all I think about is how this poem 'touched me' and answers the question 'on how I survived'! The answer sounds easier than it is, but the facts were that I had to face the fire and pain of my own feelings, stand up to grief and not choose an alternate route such as an addiction, drugs, smoking, drinking, prescription tablets or taking my own life. Some people cannot make this breakthrough for their own reason or no reason at all, but I do count myself lucky and am honored to be here today to talk about my experience. The hard work and power came from within.

I had to stand up to my fears. Feel that excruciating raw pain nearly cost my life, but now I can really say it was well worth the effort and I am proud of myself.

THE WELL OF GRIEF

Those who will not slip beneath
the still surface on the well of grief,

turning downward through its black water
to the place we cannot breathe,

will never know the source from which we drink,
the secret water, cold and clear,

nor find in the darkness glimmering,
the small round coins,
thrown by those who wished for something else.

~ David Whyte

Thank you for reading my book.

www.intimacythroughgrief.com

"May flowers always line your path and sunshine light your day.
May songbirds serenade you every step along the way.
May a rainbow run beside you in a sky that's always blue.
And may happiness fill your heart each day your whole life through".

- Irish Blessing

With Thanks

To my own family, Andre, Mom, Carl, Kim, Estelle, Roy, Neil, Jacques, Danielle, Bevan, Faye, Dominique, Matthew and Gareth and to all those family who are not with us now but stood beside us during this very hard time, you are still part of our lives and live in our hearts forever. Dezi, thanks for being such a wonderful friend and walking the final journey with me. You are very special. To our special friends John & Ann for all their help during this time and any other friends I have not mentioned, forgive me.

To Jason you are such a 'miracle' and inspiration to mankind of your challenge and pressure to survive. You made sure I was not going to lose another son as you had seen the pain it brought and you fought on regardless even though I told you not to worry about me. I am very grateful for the braveness of your choice. In all our wildest dreams we never thought this miracle would ever happen. You have taught me to fight on regardless and persevere even if in pain and if life seems like it's at the end. I hope you too will share your story with others and wait patiently for your book so that it may too inspire others.

Sarah who has gone through so many family deaths, five in your first six years of life and then watch Jason suffer his terminal illness and then miraculously survive, so desperate not to lose a second brother. You are an inspiration and I love you very much. The poem you have shared is beautiful and I hope that everyone reading this book will enjoy it too. Thank you for being my strength and having so much courage.

To everyone at Harefield & The Royal Brompton Hospital and all the Medical Staff who have been involved with Jason through the years, a very big thank you for everything.

To all my work colleagues for helping me through the second chapter of my life. You are all so dedicated to your work in nursing and I admire you for that and helping others relentlessly. To Alanda—something you said to me set off a trigger, which in turn made me write my own story which has now turned into a book! Thanks to all of you for your support!

Oriah thank you for allowing me to share your poem in my book. Your act of kindness and unselfishness has allowed me to present my story as it unfolded.

David Whyte thank you for your beautiful poetry, for your kind words and for allowing me to use 'The Well of Grief'.

My grateful thanks to all at the Waverley Chapter of Compassionate Friends, Rosemary who was my first contact for your kindness shown and letting me know that 'I need not walk alone'. Madge Rix who, in all her humanness, showed me the way. I am very grateful and wouldn't be the person I am today without your guidance, support, never ending encouragement and love. You were the 'wind beneath my wings'.

May you all be showered with blessings!

Help and Resources used

The Compassionate Friends support group for bereaved parents, family and siblings—Branches Worldwide or www.thecompassionatefriends.org

Jung and the Native American Moon Cycles: Rhythms of Influence
Michael Owen (Author)—Clinical Psychologist and Jungian Psychotherapist

Permissions

"The Invitation" by Oriah.
THE INVITATION (c) 1999.
Published by HarperONE, San Francisco. All rights reserved.
Presented with permission of the Author. www.oriah.org

'The Well of Grief', by David Whyte
'Where Many Rivers Meet' printed with permission from Many Rivers Press,
www.davidwhyte.com
©Many Rivers Press, Langley, Washington

CPSIA information can be obtained at www.ICGtesting.com
233762LV00002B/382/P